W9-DBG-464

RECOMMENDATIONS FROM AUTHORS AND THOUGHT LEADERS

"If you interested in living a more fulfilling life, Flip offers a wealth of information, strategies and techniques to do just that." **Dr. Mark Albion**, *New York Times* bestselling author, *Making a Life, Making a Living.* Dover, MA

"Flip Brown's *Balanced Effectiveness at Work* is full of big reveals. One of the most important is how to replace perfectionism and judgment with empathy and engagement. This changes everything. You'll find inspiration on every page!" **Marshall Goldsmith**, author of the *New York Times* and global bestseller *What Got You Here Won't Get You There.*

"'Flip' your conceptions about balance, with Flip Brown's thoughtful, fun, insightful book *"Balanced Effectiveness at Work."* It's pragmatic, simple yet profound, and fosters moving from speed to significance to create a more meaningful life." **Kevin Cashman**, Senior Partner, CEO and Executive Development, Korn Ferry and bestselling author, *Leadership from the Inside Out*

"Flip's approach is accessible and practical and provides a number of simple practices that will help you maintain a high level of energy at work – and at home at the end of the day. This is a useful book for any professional interested in living a healthier, more productive life." **Bryan Welch**, Publisher & Editorial Director, Ogden Publications, and author of *Beautiful and Abundant: Building the World We Want.* Topeka, KS

"How refreshing to learn that work-life balance starts within you, rather than with your over-demanding situation. Flip really makes you realize that you have control over your life and you can balance it no matter what forces come at you." **Joanie Connel**l, author of *Flying without a Helicopter: How to Prepare Young People for Work and Life.* San Diego, CA

Flip translates research, self-help, and wisdom into approachable, practical, and easy to digest steps for increasing self-awareness and effectiveness at work. This book is an invitation to grow yourself or come back to being the self you know you can be. **Arnie Kozak**, PhD., author of *Wild Chickens and Petty Tyrants: 108 Metaphors for Mindfulness.* Burlington, VT

"An eminently practical guide to creating the self-awareness needed to make positive changes, along with fun-to-read 'Flip's Tips' and down-to-earth methods for taking action. You'd be bananas not to ingest this book." **Maren Showkeir**, Co-author of *Yoga Wisdom at Work: Finding Sanity Off the Mat and On the Job.* Phoenix, AZ

"An easy-to-read format with numerous examples of those workplace people and events that make us crazy. It contains practical steps to regain control and the 'action for traction' section affords ongoing practice.." **Eileen McDargh**, CEO (Chief Energy Officer), McDargh Communications and The Resiliency Group, Dana Point, CA

"Flip packs a huge amount of information about how I can be more effective at work while keeping my cool. Even though I thought I knew a lot about this, I found out I could learn a lot more from Flip." **Julie O'Mara**, President, O'Mara and Associates. North Las Vegas, NV

"Whether nonprofit, for-profit, or self-employed, those who work to change the world tend to equate burn-out with commitment. 'Not so,' says Flip Brown, calmly and persuasively. His new book is filled with tips and tools you can apply immediately to reclaim yourself at work. Read a chapter. Take a deep breath. Read another. Breathe again. Laugh a little. Take a few notes. Now take care of yourself." **Andy Robinson**, author of *Selling Social Change (Without Selling Out)*, Plainfield, VT

"Flip shows that anyone can be a force for good at work, but only if they are balanced and effective. I wholeheartedly agree. Use this book as your roadmap to deeper success and satisfaction." **Ryan Honeyman**, author of *The B Corp Handbook: How to Use Business as a Force for Good.* San Francisco, CA

INTERNATIONAL ACCLAIM FOR
BALANCED EFFECTIVENESS AT WORK

"Packed full of witty pearls of wisdom, introspective exercises, and practical action steps, it's the perfect guide for becoming more effective, resilient and a source of positive change in the workplace." **Jessica Young**, Marketing/Communications Officer, Clean Energy Council, Melbourne, Australia

"*Balanced Effectiveness at Work* is a breath of fresh air—finally a book that prompts you to look at yourself from another person's perspective in an effort to develop a better understanding of your own dynamics and work. Well worth the read" **Shainoor Khoja**, CEO Better Business Enterprise Ltd., Dubai. United Arab Emirates

"Don't be fooled by the seemingly casual tone of *Balanced Effectiveness at Work*. This little gem of a book is full of universal and enduring wisdom that I expect will resonate as well with my clients in New Zealand as elsewhere. I recommend it highly." **Emily Morrow**, Executive Consultant. Auckland, New Zealand

"Flip has written a book I can use both personally and professionally. He combines abundant resources with personal insights to create a positive, helpful, and exciting approach." **Steve Elder**, Dipl. Psych., Cologne, Germany

"I have always believed that we control our own destiny. Buy this book. Read a chapter or two. Make some real changes. You'll have a better business and a better life." **Leen Zevenberger**, CEO, Solarus. Gälve, Sweden

"With the ever-increasing 'to-dos' in our seemingly impossible schedules, Flip's book is a must-read, offering tips and tools to help even the most harried among us achieve a more balanced way of being—both in life and at work. Don't leave home (or work) without it." **Elisa Birnbaum**, Publisher & Editor of SEE Change Magazine. Toronto, Canada

"My business is focused on one objective—'to deliver tangible and sustainable improvement to the underlying performance of any business calling on us for support.' Flip Brown provides a similar value in his own unique way to the leaders and managers he works with. His experience and wisdom is accessible to all in this book, and it has my highest recommendation." **Dave Murray**, CEO, Clive Whitegate Ltd., Cheshire, United Kingdom

PRAISE FOR
BALANCED EFFECTIVENESS AT WORK FROM BUSINESS OWNERS AND ORGANIZATION LEADERS

"Flip Brown has the formula for work life integration down to a science. His down to earth authenticity, depth, common sense, and humor make Flip an accessible, informative, and insightful read." **Joel Solomon**, Founding Partner, Renewal Funds. Vancouver, Canada

"This book provides real-life situations we can all relate to, self-reflection exercises and practical tips to get us back on track—all in an easy-to-access format written in Flip's light-hearted but sagely manner. Anyone who works, lives with or interacts with others will find loads of ideas for fine-tuning yourself and your relationships." **Amy Hall**, Director, Social Consciousness, EILEEN FISHER. Irvington, NY

"Flip takes the complicated and makes it simple. He takes the challenging, and points us in the direction of resolution and even breakthrough. By uniting his deep understanding of human motivation, his incredibly diverse experience (in work and life), and his unwavering faith in the power of compassion, Flip provides us with a roadmap to better relationships with ourselves and our work. You'll be happier and more productive, I'm sure." **Mike Rowlands**, Principal, Junxion Strategies. Vancouver, BC

"With the perfect combination of scenarios, straight forward questions, actionable tips, and access to great resources—Flip Brown has created one of the best business effectiveness guides I have ever seen. If your goal is impact with grace—this book is an essential guide. It is rare to find a smart and practical business book that is also a kick in the pants to read. Flip's combined wisdom and wit delivers the goods." **Eric Friedenwald-Fishman**, Founder/Creative Director, Metropolitan Group. Portland, OR

"This book has soul. Much more than a work/life balance 'how-to', Flip delivers guidance on how to deepen the relationships with those around us—whether co-workers or not—and the balance he describes forms the basis for how to live a more fully integrated life." **Erin Roach**, Vice-President of Marketing and Investor Relations, Farmland LP. San Francisco, CA

"*Balanced Effectiveness at Work* is a concise, jam-packed, easy to read 'how-to' guide for navigating and improving your experiences at work. Flip's compassionate and humorous prose serves to pave the to achieving greater job satisfaction, productivity and personal prosperity." **Jacquie Dragon**, Senior Vice-President of Human Resources, Merchants Bank. South Burlington, VT

"As a business owner, I've experienced Flip's coaching first-hand as he helped me grow as an effective leader and communicator. His practical approach helped me create a healthy work culture that has been good for my business and good for my employees. I'm glad to see a book that will help a wider audience benefit from his ideas." **Gregory Brand**, President, Bluehouse Group. Richmond, VT

"I am a big fan of the work that Flip Brown does and it is such a treat to have so much of his wisdom, tips and exercises contained in this book! I devoured my copy as soon as I got my hands on it, but I know that I will be referring back to the book many times in the years to come." **Carrie Russell**, Managing Director, Hospitality Valuation Services. Vancouver, BC

"Flip is engaging, authentic, full of fun and wisdom, and this book is a way for everyone to experience these qualities. It's practical, to the point, warm, compassionate and honest. This is a tool of great service to all of us who work with people...which is pretty much all of us!" **Shilpa Jain**, Executive Director, YES! Oakland, CA

"What I never learned from my Wharton MBA program but wish I had, this work is extraordinarily relevant today. Business is now beckoning our best thinking and passion in service to humanity, not just profits. Flip's work gives us the tools and encouragement to thrive by brining our full, awake, humanity to the workplace." **Steve Weinberg**, CEO, National Foundry Products, Inc. Philadelphia, PA

"I believe business is not only about the relationships you have with your co-workers, but also the one you have with yourself. Flip's unique blend of wit and wisdom provides insights, tools, and warm encouragement to an approach for finding balanced effectiveness at work. I suggest you keep a copy at your desk and by your bedside." **Ted Castle**, President, Rhino Foods. Burlington, VT

BALANCED
EFFECTIVENESS
AT WORK

**How to Enjoy the Fruits of Your Labor
without Driving Yourself Nuts**

Flip Brown

BALANCED
EFFECTIVENESS
AT WORK

**How to Enjoy the Fruits of Your Labor
without Driving Yourself Nuts**

FLIP BROWN

A USEFUL COMPENDIUM OF TIPS, TOOLS, AND
TECHNIQUES TO MAKE BEING AT WORK WORK BETTER

OPEN BOOK EDITIONS
A Berrett-Koehler Partner | iUniverse®

BALANCED EFFECTIVENESS AT WORK:
How to Enjoy the Fruits of Your Labor without Driving Yourself Nuts
www.balancedeffectiveness.com

Copyright © 2014 Flip Brown.
Produced by Business Culture Consultants

Initial cover concept and book design: Kevin Brown, Smart Set, Inc. (www.smartset.com). Cover concept revision by Jeevan Sivasubramaniam, Berrett-Koehler Publishers. Illustrations by Kim Berry Wood (licensed through iStock.com).

iUniverse books may be ordered through booksellers or by contacting:

iUniverse
1663 Liberty Drive
Bloomington, IN 47403
www.iuniverse.com
1-800-Authors (1-800-288-4677)

ISBN: 978-1-4917-4512-0 (sc)
ISBN: 978-1-4917-4511-3 (hc)
ISBN: 978-1-4917-4513-7 (e)

Library of Congress Control Number: 2014915446

Every effort has been made by the author to use 30 percent postconsumer recycled paper, Forest Sustainability Council, and/or Sustainable Forestry Initiative certified paper; however, the current level of commitment by the publishing and printing industries is such that this cannot be guaranteed. Ask about the paper in your books wherever you purchase them!

Printed in the United States of America.

iUniverse rev. date: 9/25/2014

To the one who has always been there …
Even when I haven't.
*Thanks, My (Schweetie) Pie,**
I love you so.

**Known to the rest of the world as Sandy Post*

CONTENTS

FOREWORD

Leading Social Venture Network (SVN) for the past thirteen years has been an incredible pleasure and privilege. Every day I get to connect with some of the world's leading social entrepreneurs who are collaborating to create a just and sustainable economy.

At SVN, we support whole-person leadership to help our members succeed and grow, both personally and professionally. I can't think of someone who better embodies this than Flip Brown, and I'm grateful that he has chosen to share his expertise and lessons with all of us.

Flip's experiences in business, psychology, organizational development, executive coaching, entertainment, and team facilitation have provided a rich soil for the growth of his wisdom and creativity. When he first joined our network, he quickly became one of our core members in terms of his involvement, connections, and contributions. It's clear that his primary objective is to be of service, and that commitment is clear in this book.

Working in a mission-driven business can be very rewarding, but it comes with challenges. Product and service innovation, marketing, financing, employee development, community engagement, and reduced environmental impact all require focus and balance. And no one has all the answers.

When I try too hard to "do it all and do it all well," I often end up feeling overwhelmed and scattered. Those are the best times to get clear on what's most important to me and to let go of what keeps me stuck—and those are the times when I turn to trusted advisors like Flip.

This book is like a treasure chest—the valuable lessons it offers may be experienced differently, but I can't imagine that you'll come away from reading it without turning some of its pearls of wisdom into positive change for yourself.

I can honestly say that I am enjoying more of the fruits of my labor as a result of Flip's work, and I'm resolved to be more mindful about not driving myself nuts in an attempt to do it all.

Being both balanced and effective is quite an art!

Deb Nelson, Social Venture Network, San Francisco

PREFACE

This is the book I wish someone would have handed me ten, twenty, thirty, even forty years ago. (If you're thinking, *Man, this dude is ancient!* I'll refer you to the magnet on our home refrigerator: "I may be old but at least I got to see all the cool bands"—which is basically true.)

In 2004 I was just celebrating the fourth anniversary of Business Culture Consultants, my solo practice of helping good people in great organizations have the conversations they truly need to have but haven't figured out how to have on their own yet. While I had achieved some success at that point in time, I was still riding a major roller coaster of internal and financial insecurity about whether or not I was truly going to "make it."

In 1994 I was fresh out of graduate school (and several years into living with a clean head) with my new Master's in Counseling Psychology degree. I was about to take on one of my most challenging and rewarding jobs ever—working on the Mobile Crisis Team at our community mental health center. Interacting with acutely psychotic and suicidal people on a daily basis while maintaining the required composure and compassion was a truly valuable experience; however, navigating the internal politics of a nonprofit was at times a bigger struggle.

In 1984 I was the go-to ski boot technician in a large ski shop, and in the summer I ran a windsurfing school. It was a great job, but I had this yearning for something more, and I was still practicing my world-class substance abuse behaviors. Little did I know that the following year I would move from my native Michigan to head east, eventually moving to Burlington, Vermont, to take on an executive management position in the international ski and snowboard industry, and even more stress.

In 1974 I had just moved from Gnaw Bone (no, that's not a misprint), Indiana, into the larger town of Nashville (still Indiana), and I began my apprenticeship to a skilled furniture maker. Two years later, I would open my own woodworking shop, living and working in Story, Indiana, a town

of thirteen people. And while the hippie homestead thing was great and it was a good time to be going to Grateful Dead concerts, I was fairly clueless about much of my internal world. We'll stop the history tour here.

I remember listening to James Hillman, one of my mentors, say in a workshop, "If you lived your life backwards, it would make total sense." I see now that all of my experiences—and their embedded bundles of hope and dread, joy and fear, connection and disconnection—have provided me with the raw material of this book. My burning curiosity on how to live a better, deeper, and more balanced life—personally and professionally—has been the constant rocket fuel for this astronaut's trajectory.

Sure, I've been to a lot of workshops (and given a few), read a ton of other books, and hung out with thought leaders and heart openers; however, what I've come to appreciate is that we are all on paths of our own making. Therefore, we chart our own futures.

I'm also fond of the saying "We can't or won't do something unless and until we see ourselves doing it."

Thus, while on vacation with My Pie during our annual "unplugged" trip in 2011, I typed a title on a blank page. That sat for a year, and then while staring at the sun on turquoise waters I took that title and fleshed out a preliminary chapter outline (see why you should take vacations?). But I parked that for two more years, and then when traipsing through my bulging directory of miscellaneous business files on my computer, I stumbled across the old chapter outline. *Hmm, not bad*, I thought.

On March 13, 2014, I received an e-mail from a good man by the name of Mal Warwick (legendary in several circles) with the subject line "So, You Want to Write a Book?" This was an invitation to sign up for a workshop at the Social Venture Network Spring Conference with Marvelous Mal and a certain Mr. Steve Piersanti, the President of Berrett-Koehler Publishers, *the* leading publisher of books for the socially responsible business community and, like Business Culture Consultants (my humble one-person company), an allied Certified B Corp.

This serendipitous e-mail landed in my mailbox the very day that I was headed to the Esalen Institute in Big Sur, California, for a personal retreat. Sitting there on the West Coast, looking out at the waves crashing into the shore below, with the sounds of a waterfall behind me and the warm California sun on my shoulders, I experienced one of those good,

old-fashioned body rushes that we have from time to time when every cell in our bodies becomes aware that we are at a significant junction. At that point I realized that *now* was the time for me to assemble some of the humble wisdom I had collected and generated in my work, and give it a form so it could potentially be of service to others. I wrote the first eight chapters there and then.

Since I now had the picture of what the book was going to be, I created it and delivered an edited manuscript to the publisher four months to the day from when I made the decision to do it. In case you have any doubt, you too can take your thoughts of an imagined future and bring them into the reality that is your life.

I hope you enjoy this little collection of the fruits of my labor. Heaven knows I had plenty of occasions to drive myself nuts along the way.

Flip Brown

•

ACKNOWLEDGMENTS

Ah, where to start in terms of expressing my gratitude, which runs deep and wide. First, as the dedication states, I would not be able to take on a project of this scope and commitment without the love and support of my life partner, Sandy. She wants the best for me, and she also wants the best from me. Her faith in my ability to get out of my own way (and therefore be more present with her) has been a major positive force in my life.

I thank my brother, Kevin, not only for his work on this book but also for being my one true brother. With my sister Pam, we support and challenge each other, and along with my other sister Cheryl, we carry on the legacy of our parents, who are now in spirit. I am appreciative of the love of learning I received from my mother; and the strong work ethic, the components of customer service, and the workplace values I obtained from my father. I also thank the Elder family for their caring and support.

My business would not be what it is today without the wonderful members of our Vermont business community. I am grateful to have served on the Board of Vermont Businesses for Social Responsibility from 2002 to 2011, and to remain connected to the largest organization of its kind in North America. I love our unique—yes, quirky—way of engaging in business here, with a focus on being local, green (literally and figuratively), and compassionate.

My personal and professional lives have changed in significantly positive ways through being a Member of the Social Venture Network. Deb Nelson, the Executive Director, not only does an awesome job, but she has been an avid supporter and friend. A special note of profound appreciation goes out to my SVN Peer Circle—Amy Hall, Shainoor Khoja, Libba Pinchot, Mike Rowlands, and Steve Weinberg. As I often say, I would have to be in the hospital or in jail to miss our monthly highly supportive and interactive calls.

Having my business become a Certified B Corp has been invaluable from a "walk my talk" perspective, as well as bringing me into another amazing community. I appreciate Jay, Bart, and Andrew—the Founders—and the staff there as well for all they do at B Lab.

I'm grateful for the teachers in my meditation tradition—Dan, George, Susan, Gretchen, and John—who have helped me with seeing things through the perspective of "not self" and providing me with a practice.

One of the major ways in which I recharge my batteries is through music, and for eighteen years I've been playing with my fellow musicians—Jeff Marble, Bill Gardner, Greg Farkas, and Bart Merle-Smith—in the Retro Rockets, as well as other musicians who I jam with. Rock on, indeed!

I have so many colleagues who are part of my "virtual team" that I cannot possibly list them all. For all those in my network, I express my thanks.

Clearly, some of my best teachers have been my wonderful clients, who, over the past twenty years, have questioned me, laughed with (and sometimes at) me, and shared poignant moments of growth and change. I continue to learn, earn, and grow through the opportunity to be of service.

This book would not have come to fruition without the interest and support of the teams at Berrett-Koehler Publishing and iUniverse. Specifically, Steve Piersanti's original invitation to meet with him in B-K's San Francisco office opened the door. Johanna Vondeling and Jeevan Sivasubramanim provided excellent connections and service. This led me to sign a contract for the Open Book Editions program, a Berrett-Koehler partnership with iUniverse (located in Bloomington, Indiana—the site of the first ski shop I worked in!). Special thanks go to Adalee Cooney as the helpful production chief, and Jess Jacobs for her skillful project management at iUniverse. In addition, I'd like to thank Nic Albert for developmental editing, Kelsye Nelson for superb platform and launch services, and Mark Levy for conceptual mind expansion.

A very special thanks goes out to Olivia Vande Griek, my superbly talented research assistant. She will go far on her path, however it unfolds.

And finally, I wish to express my gratitude to the Universal Life Force, the "awakened awareness," that mystery that is beyond total comprehension and description, summed up for me in a lyric from John Lennon:

"Limitless, undying love which shines around me like a million suns—it calls me on and on, across the universe."

INTRODUCTION

See if this fits your experience in any way: you're commuting in to work in the morning, and in your head you begin the daily ritual of prioritizing your upcoming workday. You go over that mental sticky note with your urgent to-dos, and you see that there are three to five *absolutely crucial things* that you must accomplish today.

Fast-forward to the commute home. You realize that not only did you not get all of those hot-button items accomplished today, *but you added three to five more extremely important items to the list.*

This is what I call being "swept along." When this happens, our experience can vary from mild irritation, to hope that someday we'll "get on top of things," to a consistent sense of inadequacy. None of these are optimal states of being.

This is just one of the ways in which we drive ourselves nuts. I know I'm at risk for telling warm and fuzzy stories about the Best Days of the Boomers (which, in the case of rock 'n' roll, are often true!). However, there was a time not too long ago with less complexity. When we were alone, we were truly alone, because we didn't have these amazing Star Trek transponders going off in our pockets. When we were in a group, we were looking at each other or staring off in space, but we weren't sending and receiving god-knows-what on little screens.

Life at work takes the basic complexity of your current job, and adds outputs, budgets, work flow, meetings, politics, pressure, and deadlines. And this is on a normal day. What we often lack—or forget—is an inner sense of the reasonable, functional, and centered options to deal with the stresses of work. So, during the day, there are either infrequent spurts of satisfaction, or we delay having a sense of our whole being until we are away from work (although these same patterns can and do show up there too).

My hope is that the reader finds the material here to be "news you can use" in a realistic, practical way. Since we are all renting physical bodies for a very limited time, why not be as alive, centered, and content as possible? I wish you the best in enjoying your full potential, however that unfolds for you personally and professionally.

HOW TO USE THIS BOOK

Each of the twenty-four chapters uses the same structure, outlined below. While the chapters are built around eight sequential sections, you should be able to open the book to any chapter and find value.

a. *Opening quote:* A selected bit of wit or wisdom designed to set the tone.
b. *What it is ...* A concise description of what the chapter title means.
c. *Sample scenario #1:* A vignette of one or more characters in a fictional workplace setting to provide an example.
d. *Sample scenario #2:* An example that offers a different element or style of the chapter topic.
e. *Why will this help me at work?* A tie-in to the workplace, to keep the focus on being effective at work, rather than just "self-help."
f. *Why is this so difficult at times?* An exploration of the challenges at hand (otherwise, if all this were so easy, you wouldn't be looking at this book!).
g. *Your frank self-assessment:* Three questions that invite the reader to look at his or her own patterns.
h. *Flip's tips:* My suggestions about how to initiate a change process in this area.
i. *Action for traction:* Specific, concrete things to do in order to have a different experience over time.
j. *Baked-in benefits:* A positive reinforcement of the goodies that the reader will get by making a commitment and following through.
k. *For a deeper dive ...* Additional print resources for further exploration.
l. *... and on the Web:* Online options of value.
m. *Notes and Noodlings:* Space for your thoughts.

For current information, additional resources, and other relevant musings, please visit this book's website: www.balancedeffectiveness.com

Thanks for your interest!

SECTION ONE

Self-as-Construct
(Or, You Built Who You Are
So You Can Remodel Yourself!)

CHAPTER 1

It's All About You (But Then Again, It's Not Really)

"People often say that this or that person has not yet found himself.
But the self is not something one finds, it is something one creates."
—THOMAS SZASZ

What it is … The next time you're bummed out about your past, current, or future situation, there is a powerful tool that can show you where the answers reside—and I'm sure you have one in your office or home. It's called a mirror! How we view ourselves and the options we have to change is fundamental to our success and satisfaction. The bottom line is that you *can* do something about your situation, even if you temporarily believe otherwise.

Sample scenario #1: Akiko loves to complain and is gifted in telling anyone (who will listen) about how dire her circumstances are, even though she has an interesting job, a good salary, good health, and people who care about her. When challenged about her "finding the dark lining in every cloud," she shrugs it off, saying, "If I didn't point out what's not working, who would?" Needless to say, her coworkers give her a wide berth.

Sample scenario #2: Warren always has a smile and a kind word for everyone, and frequently makes positive contributions to the group process. Very few people know that Warren has a chronic medical condition that requires careful monitoring, that he cares for his eighty-four-year-old mother in the beginning stages of Alzheimer's dementia, and that he financially provides for a son with a mental health diagnosis who lives out of state. How can he be so consistently pleasant?

Why will this help me at work? How we view ourselves and then exercise our options as we move through the stress of the workplace is a primary determinant of our experience (as well as for those around us). If we are looking for ways to make it better and improve the situation, it is more

likely that we can and will. Reducing our negativity will have an infectious, positive impact on those around us.

Why is this so difficult at times? Taking responsibility for ourselves sounds like something we all should do without grumbling. However, for most of us, there are a variety of reasons why this is hard. These include: the patterns we inherited from our families, working in toxic organizational cultures, lack of emotional intelligence, and the "feel-good" of making someone else responsible (to name a few!).

Your frank self-assessment:
- Has the world given you a series of challenging opportunities, or has it stacked the deck against you?
- What are your beliefs about your ability to control your destiny?
- Do you hang out with people who are positive beings, or do they reinforce pettiness, blaming others, and general conspiracy theories?

Flip's tips:
- Begin to practice being the neutral "observer" of your day. Try recording your thoughts and inner feelings to see how much self-doubt and procrastination are part of the background. For now, just observe (and make a few notes if you like).
- Think about your heroes and other people you admire. Why do they inspire you? How do you see yourself in them? By emulating people we admire, we can internalize different ways of "viewing and doing" in the world.
- Think about the first steps you would take if you truly had the ability to change your world for the positive. Make a list of the things you can do that don't require those around you to agree with you or to give you permission.

Action for traction:
- Write the (abbreviated) story of your life so far in two versions—the first where you have emerged from your circumstances to be an average modern superhero with special powers, and the second, a modern tragedy where life's dramas have kept you from riches and happiness. Go ahead and exaggerate. Which one feels more like your true story?

- Ask the people you trust to rate you on a scale of one (low) to ten (high) on optimism. If you're surprised by the results, see if you can figure out how they came to their conclusions.
- List the top ten positive changes that you have made in your life, and then the next top ten you are going to make. Spend some time visualizing what it will look and feel like once you do so.

Baked-in benefits:
- We directly increase our self-confidence, not from the basis of our ego, but from quiet acceptance of our basic goodness.
- By understanding that we always have options (even though they may not be obvious or the ones we immediately want), we tend to reduce our feelings of hopelessness or cynicism.
- If we want those around us to be creative, energetic, enthusiastic, and positive, there's no better place to start than by the good old "be the change you want to see."

For a deeper dive ...
Albion, Mark. *True to Yourself: Leading a Values-Based Business.* San Francisco: Berrett-Koehler Publishers, 2006.

Ben-Shahar, Tal. *Happier: Learn the Secrets to Daily Joy and Lasting Fulfillment.* New York: McGraw-Hill, 2007.

... and on the Web:
Firestone, Lisa. "7 Steps to Living the Life You Imagined." *Psychology Today.* May 16, 2013. Accessed August 2, 2014. http://www.psychologytoday.com/collections/201405/stay-positive/7-steps-living-the-life-you-imagined

Gilbert, Dan. "The Surprising Science of Happiness." TED Talks. February 2004. Accessed August 2, 2014. http://www.ted.com/talks/dan_gilbert_asks_why_are_we_happy

NOTES AND NOODLINGS

CHAPTER 2

Your Personality—Friend or Enemy?
(The Answer Is Yes!)

*"I'm successful because of my personality ... but
I'm also successful in spite of my personality."*
—UNKNOWN, BUT ONE OF MY FAVORITES

What it is ... One way to describe our personality is to say that it is made up of our patterns of thinking, feeling, and behaving. When we show up at work, we are bringing these patterns with us, and to the extent that they are useful, we can be successful. To the degree that these patterns create blind spots, cause disconnects, and keep us from succeeding, we need a means to understand them and then ways to create change.

Sample scenario #1: Demarco is a very accommodating dude. Known for his easygoing manner, he believes that getting along with everyone has the highest value. Problem is, Demarco frequently finds himself not getting what he needs at work because he does not take an assertive stance.

Sample scenario #2: Ethel has no problems letting anyone know just exactly what she thinks or what she feels. While her frank statements and candid sharing can be refreshing, she often fails to notice when others need space, or that her timing can be off.

Why will this help me at work? If you're not aware of your personality and its patterns, then you are at risk for being less effective, for projecting your unresolved muck onto others, for finding fault and blame with those around you, and for feeling like you have no good options. When we focus on what we can do to improve ourselves, not only do we get better, but we also serve to model exactly the behavior and approach we want to experience from others. Funny how that works!

Why is this so difficult at times? The very patterns that can serve us well sometimes can be overutilized in situations where another response would work better. However, we still cling to those patterns because of the successes they've brought us in the past. Demarco gets high marks for his relaxed style. Ethel's candor is appreciated at times. If it works, why look at it differently or change it? Given various situations, we need a variety of responses to be effective, but we may not have had the opportunity to see new ways and practice them.

Your frank self-assessment:
- What are the patterns that have created difficulties for you in the past?
- Do "automatic responses" emerge that you wish you could temper or adjust?
- Where have you received either supportive or harsh feedback about your blind spots?

Flip's tips:
- Check out one of the popular assessment instruments, like the Myers-Briggs Type Indicator© or DISC© to have a reference point on your personality type. Keep in mind, though, that we don't all fit neatly into sixteen boxes of personality types. These tools are a starting point, not an ending one.
- Google "Johari's Window." Find a trusted colleague or friend who knows you at work to provide you with honest feedback on what your "Hidden Self" and "Unknown Self" look like to her.
- Go on a "listening tour," where you ask colleagues, coworkers, and (if you dare) family members something along the lines of "If you observe things that I do that inadvertently have a negative impact on our relationship, or keep me from getting what I need, would you be willing to share those perceptions with me?"

Action for traction:
- If you had a magic wand and you could modify three elements of your personality so that you could be more effective at work, what would they be? Take one element from your "magic wand" list, and without negative judgment, track how often it shows up in a week by simply observing it as it occurs.
- Set up some reminders for yourself so that you can be more aware in the moment (e.g., "When I start fidgeting in my chair, it means that I am becoming impatient and don't want to listen anymore").

- What are the specific choices you can make in terms of how to do things differently once you have that awareness? ("I can find a way to truly listen to the other and not be so impatient.")

Baked-in benefits:
- We have the direct experience that we are not "swept along" by our old unhelpful patterns.
- We provide positive modeling to others to look at and take responsibility for their contributions.
- We reinforce our own commitment to growth and change.

For a deeper dive …
Lombardo, Michael. *FYI: For Your Improvement—For Learners, Managers, Mentors, and Feedback Givers.* 5th ed. Minneapolis, MN: Lominger International, 2009.

Myers, Isabella Briggs, and Peter Myers. *Gifts Differing: Understanding Personality Types.* Boston: Nicolas Brealey America, 1995.

… and on the Web:
Huffington Post. "The Third Metric—Redefining Success Beyond Money & Power." August 2, 2014. Accessed August 2, 2014. http://www.huffingtonpost.com/news/third-metric/

Madell, Robin. "Can You Be Yourself at Work?" *Huffington Post.* September 26, 2013. Accessed August 2, 2014. http://www.huffingtonpost.com/2013/09/26/personality-at-work_n_3976087.html

Reinhold, Ross. "Personality Pathways: Exploring Personality Type & Its Applications." July 22, 2014. Accessed August 2, 2014. http://www.personalitypathways.com/

NOTES AND NOODLINGS

CHAPTER 3

Your Family of Origin (Hopefully) Doesn't Work Here—Getting the Patterns of the Past Out of the Present

"If you cannot get rid of the family skeleton,
you may as well make it dance."
—GEORGE BERNARD SHAW

What it is ... We'd like to think that we're fully grown, that we took the good and left the bad behind when we set out on our own as adults. The reality is that there are patterns of thinking, feeling, and behaving outside of our conscious awareness that we have adopted. When these show up in our work relationships, they can sometimes cause tension, blame, or disconnection. Our opportunity and responsibility is to understand and work through these dynamics—both our positive legacies and any unwanted negative ones.

Sample scenario #1: Peggy is great at what she does, and cranks out a high volume of accurate work. However, when her male supervisor comes up behind her and looks over her shoulder, she silently fumes. *Why doesn't he trust me to get my work done?* she thinks. *I wish he would go about his own business and stop micromanaging me.* She confides in a coworker, who doesn't really see the problem with the boss stopping by, especially since it's almost always complimentary. In a session with her executive coach, Peggy realizes that her father, who was a university professor, used to come stand behind her and negatively scrutinize her homework.

Sample scenario #2: Toshiro appears to be a crabby workaholic. He is often holed up in his office, "too busy" to take routine questions and engage in normal conversations with teammates. He comes early, leaves late, and takes several fat files home in his briefcase every night. When his supervisor confronts him in a supportive way, telling him that he needs to

work smarter, not harder, Toshiro's face gets red and he stammers, "Can't you see that this company is going to go under unless we all put in our best effort?" Toshiro has yet to discover that he is unconsciously mimicking his father, whose seventy- to eighty-hour workweeks could not save their small family business from bankruptcy.

Why will this help me at work? If we are projecting our unresolved family-of-origin conflicts, hidden feelings, and old worn-out roles into our business interactions, we are not accurately dealing with the present reality. When people describe the environment where they work with the phrase "It's just like family," I am tempted to say, "Look out!" even though I know what their intention is. Show me a family that has truly worked out its power dynamics, created a mutual feeling of fairness, has a functional decision-making process, and does equitable financial distributions, and I'll give you a small prize!

Why is this so difficult at times? How we originally encoded our ways of making sense of the world—including family tensions, strong negativity, and even abusive situations—was outside our conscious process. For example, we didn't choose to list our options and then decide to be a perfectionist as a child because we were living in a chaotic environment and thought that if we became a control freak it would help everyone out. Bringing these patterns into our awareness is difficult. This is because the very definition of the unconscious is that we are not able to always understand what we are doing and why, since that information is not available to our normal capabilities. Therefore almost every single successful businessperson I know today has been through some experience of psychotherapy, to make sure that he or she is not being hijacked by old dramas.

Your frank self-assessment:
- Write down the positive attributes that you received from your family. Without fault or blame, list the elements that have been problematic.
- Have you received any feedback (often from a caring spouse or partner) that you sometimes act in ways that are "not yourself?"
- What is your mixture of joy and resentment, of success and failure, and of pride and shame when you talk about what it was like for you growing up?

Flip's tips:
- Make sure this doesn't turn into parent or family "bashing"—people almost always did the best they could given their level of awareness at the time.
- Just because we are aware of something doesn't mean that we can instantly change it. Be patient with yourself.
- If you decide that some old personal patterns are creating a negative impact at work and you want to find someone to work with, initiate the courageous conversation to inquire among your friends and colleagues whom they might recommend (more folks have been to counseling than you might think). Asking for help is a sign of strength, not weakness.

Action for traction:
- Pick one pattern that you are fairly sure comes from your past, and simply track it. For example, if you tend to freeze up when anyone else at work raises his or her voice, simply take note when this happens. See if this increases your ability to think of options when this occurs.
- Take a story that you have told yourself about someone at work, and put this into the context of your family. See any strong similarities? This could indicate a need for you to rewrite that tale to reflect your current work-based situation.
- Are there any needs that your current employer or supervisor is not meeting for you? List these, and then see which ones may be realistic in an actual business environment (e.g., "I want to understand if there is a path here for my professional advancement") versus historical (e.g., "I'm never seen for the contributions I make around here").

Baked-in benefits:
- When we can see how our old patterns create responses that aren't tied to the current situation, we can free up enormous energy for engagement and connection.
- By recognizing our triggers, we can compassionately engage with others by taking responsibility.
- We benefit not only from clearing out the negative historical components, but by accentuating the positive as well. From my father, I got some unhelpful moody tendencies to withdraw at times, but I also received a strong work ethic. From my mother, I

inherited a tendency to intellectualize when it may not be helpful; however, I also was blessed with a lifelong love of learning.

For a deeper dive …
Miller, Alice. *Drama of the Gifted Child: The Search for the True Self.* rev. ed. New York: Basic Books, 1996.

Richo, David. *When the Past Is Present: Healing the Emotional Wounds That Sabotage Our Relationships.* Boston: Shambala, 2008.

… and on the Web:
Babuta, Leo. "Regret." Zen Habits. June 16, 2014. Accessed August 2, 2014. http://zenhabits.net/regret//

Brenner, Gail. "10 Smart Choices to Heal the Pain of Your Past." *The Change Blog.* June 15, 2014. Accessed August 2, 2014. http://www.thechangeblog.com/heal-pain-past/

Clemens, Peter. *The Change Blog.* July 31, 2014. Accessed August 2, 2014. http://www.thechangeblog.com/

NOTES AND NOODLINGS

SECTION TWO

Self-Talk—Changing the Invisible
Ways in Which We Sustain
Our Own Delicious Delusions

CHAPTER 4

How Dare You Speak to Yourself Like That?—Examining Our Internal Dialogue

"View your life with kindsight. Stop beating yourself up about things from your past. Instead of slapping your forehead and asking, 'What was I thinking,' breathe and ask yourself the kinder question, 'What was I learning?'"
—KAREN SALMANSOHN

What it is ... We have an astonishing capacity to set unreasonably high internal standards, look for the slightest evidence that we may in fact be screwing up, and serve as judge and jury for ourselves, usually with a "guilty" verdict. What happens too often is that the capacity for compassionate self-evaluation is overshadowed by an unrealistic, incessant inner negativity.

Sample scenario #1: Aailyah has a running voice inside her head that says she should somehow be doing more, in spite of a demanding job, three kids at home, an ailing mother, and her volunteer work in the community. Others give her regular accolades for her positive energy, yet Aailyah often lies awake at night or stares off in the distance during the day, wondering in a vague sense *What's wrong with me that I can't do better?*

Sample scenario #2: Charles heaps praise upon his direct reports, has a kind word for the other department managers, and is authentically pleasant with his boss. However, it is well-known that if you walk by his office and the door is open, you can frequently hear him muttering phrases like "You stupid idiot" and "Nice work, knucklehead" to himself.

Why will this help me at work? Even though we may mask it well, our negative internal dialogue still has its effects. First, we often project our unnecessary frustration onto others, frequently without our awareness as it's happening. Secondly, we may be perceived as "moody" as we go through our rituals of self-recrimination, and this reduces our availability to others.

Third, this is another example of the benefits of modeling the positive behavior we want to see from others.

Why is this so difficult at times? Here's a little bit of psychological theory for you. When we were kids and there was tension or significant unmet needs in our environment, we didn't have a lot of choices. We certainly couldn't say at the age of six or ten, "Hey, I'm going to go get a job and an apartment, and I'll check back in with you." One response for us was to "be bad," but that came with some big trade-offs (like "ouch!"). So many of us internalized the sentiment that "if something is wrong, maybe it's because I'm not doing the right thing." This potentially sets us up for a lifetime of trying to be OK, when in fact, we already are.

Your frank self-assessment:
- You may not know how much of this lies within. What are some negative thoughts, feelings, or statements that you have had about yourself? Take a pad or pile of blank cards, and in three minutes, write down quickly, without censorship, every negative thought, feeling, or statement you've ever had or made about yourself. If you're like me (when I did this exercise in a workshop), you may be stunned at what you capture.
- What are the primary themes or statements that you tell yourself when things aren't going well? If they are self-critical, how can you reframe them?
- Who are your allies—the people who can see through the false assessments and stern admonitions to support you? Can you tap in to them and their positive mirroring more often?

Flip's tips:
- If you have a harsh inner critic, know that you're not alone. It is amazing to me that once I develop a sense of trust with the people I work with, a gentle line of questioning will almost always reveal that the person I'm talking to has this dynamic as well.
- There are two manifestations of this pattern that have labels— one is "caretaker," where we are hard on ourselves because we unrealistically feel that everyone around us should be okay first, and the second is "perfectionist," where nothing is right with us unless and until it is perfectly right.
- Either unpack those old bags or leave them at the curb, but don't drag them along. There's almost always a family history component in this dynamic. Sometimes it's useful to understand

how the pattern got there, and sometimes it's just helpful to focus on changing it.

Action for traction:
- What are the primary themes or statements that you tell yourself when things aren't going well? Go to extremes—write down a description, as if you were writing a novel, of this most despicable character that you see when you look in the mirror. Go ahead and list all of the truly bad habits, huge deficiencies, and glaring gaps. Now, have a good laugh.
- The ones you love must know. Give those closest to you the permission to share what they've seen or heard in terms of your self-judgment. Take it as their investment in your well-being.
- Do you have the "roller-coaster effect"—one day you're brilliant and on top of the world, an hour or day later you're lower than whale poop? These cycles make it hard to be balanced, so notice what happens as it's happening and then use that awareness to even things out in the moment.

Baked-in benefits:
- By demonstrating more empathy, compassion, and acceptance toward yourself, you'll be in a better place to give the same to others.
- You'll provide a valuable service to your children, anyone that you mentor, and those around you who struggle with the same dynamic.
- You'll appear less neurotic. How delightful!

For a deeper dive …
Brown, Brené. *The Gifts of Imperfection: Let Go of Who You Think You're Supposed to Be and Embrace Who You Are.* Center City, MN: Hazelden, 2010.

Firestone, Robert W., Lisa Firestone, and Joyce Catlett. *Conquer Your Critical Inner Voice: A Revolutionary Program to Counter Negative Thoughts and Live Free from Imagined Limitations.* Oakland, CA: New Harbinger, 2002.

… and on the Web:
Becker-Phelps, Leslie. "How to Stop the Self-Criticism and Feel Better About You." *Psychology Today.* July 27, 2011. Accessed August 2, 2014.

http://www.psychologytoday.com/blog/making-change/201107/
how-stop-the-self-criticism-and-feel-better-about-you

Deschene, Lori. "5 Ways to Validate Yourself: Be Part of Your Support System." *Tiny Buddha*. Accessed August 2, 2014. http://tinybuddha.com/blog/5-ways-to-validate-be-part-of-your-support-system/

Mind Tools. "The ABC Technique: Overcoming Pessimistic Thinking." Accessed August 2, 2014. http://www.mindtools.com/pages/article/abc.htm

NOTES AND NOODLINGS

CHAPTER 5

Go Ahead and Worry—It Will Solve Everything!

"The greatest mistake you can make in life is to
be continually fearing you will make one."
—ELBERT HUBBARD

What it is ... Fear, and its smaller sibling—anxiety—can serve a useful purpose in our lives, but only in a very narrow way, and under specific circumstances. Most of what we hold as anxiety about the workplace falls under the old-fashioned category of "neurotic": it's not really significant enough to require any drastic action, and it's usually about our inability to keep ourselves centered and balanced.

Sample scenario #1: Sally worries that she'll disappoint her team if she doesn't stop at the bakery every Friday to pick up goodies. She's concerned about what her manager will think if she makes a mistake. Her coworkers will roll their eyes in a meeting when Sally asks yet another question just so she can "get it right." Her to-do lists are massive, and there's always one more thing to add.

Sample scenario #2: Deion doesn't consider himself to be a suspicious person; however he does have his doubts about where the owners are taking the company, whether that new young buck is after his job, and what his supervisor meant in that last e-mail. He is concerned that he may find himself without a job, so he spends much time documenting his actions, which he considers to be simply "covering my ass."

Why will this help me at work? Whether you worry about too many details, are anxious about the future, or are overly concerned about what people think of you, you are robbing your present of available time and energy. Appropriate concern is good; obsessing on what might or should happen is not. Others in the workplace tend to create work-arounds rather than dealing openly with a "nervous Nelson or Nellie."

Why is this so difficult at times? For most people with an anxious personality component, the worry is an attempt to self-soothe. If "out of control" is the worst thing that can happen (and sometimes it's actually quite desirable to move skillfully through out of control), then being wigged out may try to serve a purpose of managing a negative internal state. When you do not have trust in your own capacity to go into the unknown, then dealing with ambiguity will be a supreme challenge.

Your frank self-assessment:
- Has anyone ever referred to you as a "control freak"? A "worrywart"? Is there any potential truth to this?
- Are you able to sit quietly and contemplate your next moves, or is there usually an internal pressure to figure it out and get it done right now?
- Do you beat yourself up for not getting enough accomplished? Do you have an incessant feeling that you should be doing more?

Flip's tips:
- If this is a pattern for you, it could be a challenging one to change. You'll have to replace being worried with accepting "what is" (without turning into a complacent blob of jelly!).
- Ask yourself this question: "Is it possible for me to do more than the best I can do?" Now, make sure you right-size "best."
- Identify the ways you differentiate between concern and worry, or between being focused and being obsessed. Make sure you can pick up the internal feeling of "being okay" versus "not being okay."

Action for traction:
- See if you can figure out—with a trusted friend, colleague, or counselor—what is at the root of your anxiety. Knowing the basis behind it won't automatically make it disappear, but it could provide some understanding.
- Using the 1–10 scale, with 10 being something like nuclear war, 9 being brutal violence or murder, 8 being the death of someone very close to you, 7 being a diagnosis of a terminal illness, and so on, it's easy to see that the things we think are major episodes of disaster in the workplace are in fact 2s and 3s. Make up your own scale and keep track of how many times you initially perceive a 3 to be an 8.
- Practice talking privately to yourself in a mirror. Tell yourself exactly why things are so dire, the horrible outcomes you are imagining, and the absolutely heroic efforts you and only you

must take in order to stave off catastrophe. See how long you can keep this up!

Baked-in benefits:
- Bringing the triggers for your own anxiety into your awareness and changing them will have major positive impacts on the ones you truly care about. Loving an uptight person (that would be you) is not an easy task.
- Ironically, the less you truly obsess over details, the more likely you are to be seen as highly valuable. Think about it—are the leaders you admire calm or chaotic?
- Yes, there are folks who get their work done, hang out with good friends, and enjoy a rich full life, but they don't take a checklist approach to it. Use focused concern as a tool, not a burden.

For a deeper dive …
Bourne, Edmund J. *The Anxiety and Phobia Workbook.* 5th ed. Oakland, CA: New Harbinger Publications, 2011.

Hallowell, Edward M. *Worry.* New York: Ballantine, 1998.

… and on the Web:
Freedom from Fear. "Anxiety and Depression Resource Site." Accessed August 2, 2014. http://www.freedomfromfear.org/

McGonigal, Kelly. "How to Make Stress Your Friend." TED Talks. June 2013. Accessed August 2, 2014. http://www.ted.com/talks/kelly_mcgonigal_how_to_make_stress_your_friend

We Worry: A Blog for the Anxious. http://weworry.wordpress.com/

NOTES AND NOODLINGS

CHAPTER 6

But What About Time Management? (How About Energy Management Instead?)

"Beware the barrenness of a busy life."
—SOCRATES

What it is … Many of us create unrealistic expectations about how many tasks and accomplishments we can fit into a single business day. We seem to continually search for ways to deal with the pressure of lists, meetings, deadlines, and commitments. Meanwhile, the stress of trying to keep up with this mess actually reduces our productivity.

Sample scenario #1: Sam is always three to seven minutes late, forgets to eat, and the last time he took a vacation he responded to e-mails and calls from the office for several hours each day. He went to a time-management seminar and bought some software that was supposed to link everything together, but nothing has really changed. He dreams that someday he'll buy a llama farm in Vermont.

Sample scenario #2: Nancy seems to have a gap between how much she believes she can simultaneously juggle, and her actual output. When someone at work asks her if she can deliver a certain packet of data, she has a tendency to respond, "Uh … yeah, I'll get that to you by noon on Friday," and this has happened so often (without the actual delivery) that new employees are unfairly set up to put in a request to see if the response will be the same from "noon-on-Friday Nancy."

Why will this help me at work? This one is another "BFO" (Blinding Flash of the Obvious) in that it is often the perceived demands of work that cause us to get bunched up in our undies. I have seen and worked with folks who move through their days with reasonable grace and composure, and their workloads and responsibilities are no less than yours. The less time we

spend thinking about what we are going to do because we have too much to do, the more we can actually get done.

Why is this so difficult at times? First, the key to understanding this topic—as the chapter title says—is to shift from "time management" to "energy management." Our experience of time is not actually as a rigid, fixed quantity ticking by, but as a fluid element. When you're in love or playing with your grandkid or skiing in the perfect snow, time is elastic and flowing. When you're stuck in that boring operations meeting again, every second drags. The other main challenge is that in planning each day, we forget to allow for the unexpected. There will always be things that cannot be anticipated in advance, but we don't allow ourselves space or permission for these events.

Your frank self-assessment:
- Do you keep searching for the perfect or better system that will someday magically keep you on track? How's that working so far?
- Are you able to accept that there are limits to what can be done, and that it's up to you to set them (or find a more reasonable workplace culture)?
- Do you take realistic breaks, or do you believe that Superwoman and Superman don't need these because they have super powers?

Flip's tips:
- Technology is often not our friend. Use the same standard for e-mail that you would for paper: is this something that I want to keep around and keep track of? In about 98 percent of the time, the answer is "no," so send it to your Trash, and set your Trash to delete anything over thirty days each day. If it's worth saving, then save it now. Otherwise, if it's a month old and you haven't had to dig it out of the Trash, let it go.
- Make sure you periodically take as much time as you can—a minimum of forty-eight hours, seven full days is better—for a regular "digital detox." When we unplug our devices, we return to a more natural rhythm—the one that life is based on, actually. You'll be surprised how well the world gets along without you.
- When you have to choose between what ultimately is a positive set of feelings (playing ball with your kid, walking out of the gym) versus a crummy or ho-hum set of feelings (like taking another hour to do vague research on the Internet), imagine yourself an hour from now. Determine which set of feelings is going to

contribute more to your feeling recharged and resilient, and let that be your motivator.

Action for traction:
- You make appointments with other people and keep them, don't you? Make that same firm commitment with yourself: write into your calendar (and if it's a shared work calendar, so much the better) things like "10:00 a.m.—Project Completion Meeting with F. Brown (only)" or "4:30 p.m.—Senior Services Manager (that's you) out for Health Improvement Project (that's the gym)."
- Take your current to-do list, and find the 10 or 20 percent of the items that—if you're serious—just aren't going to happen anytime soon. Put them on a "List of Future Possibilities" and stick that list in your drawer for three months. Then, see if they're still important.
- Choose an accountability buddy. If you tend to eat lunch at your desk in a vain attempt to get more done, give him or her the permission to "bust" you and get you to sit in the lunchroom and connect face-to-face. Often, investing in our relationships creates higher value than the creation of another spreadsheet.

Baked-in benefits:
- Developing more realistic expectations leads to less stress, better balance, more focus, and higher-quality output.
- You'll serve as a role model for others (or at least get them wondering what the heck's gotten into you!)
- This one works at home too!

For a deeper dive …
Allen, David. *Getting Things Done: The Art of Stress-Free Productivity.* New York: Penguin Books, 2002.

Stack, Laura. *What to Do When There's Too Much to Do: Reduce Tasks, Increase Results, and Save 90 Minutes a Day.* Oakland, CA: Berrett-Koehler Publishers, 2012.

… and on the Web:
Bates, Jordan. "Psych Basics: Time Management." *Psychology Today.* http://www.psychologytoday.com/basics/time-management

Mueller, Annie. *Freakishly Productive.* Accessed August 2, 2014. http://freakishlyproductive.com/

"Work Smarter, Not Harder: 21 Time Management Tips to Hack Productivity." *Refine the Mind Blog.* Accessed August 2, 2014. http://www.refinethemind.com/21-time-management-tips//

NOTES AND NOODLINGS

SECTION THREE

Self-in-Relationship—
You Mean I Have to Play
Well with Others?

CHAPTER 7

Really? That's What You Meant?— The Importance of Shared Definitions, Expectations, and Assumptions

"We are now at a point in time when the ability to receive, utilize, store, transform and transmit data—the lowest cognitive form—has expanded literally beyond comprehension. Understanding and wisdom are largely forgotten as we struggle under an avalanche of data and information."
—DEE HOCK

What it is ... So often in the workplace, we think that everyone is relatively on the same page; however, it is probably more accurate to assume that it's like the bar scene from the first *Star Wars* movie—aliens from every different galaxy, each with their own conceptual frameworks and languages (not to mention ray guns!). Unless we take the time to really get a sense of whether or not we are working from some common ground, we can frequently find ourselves at odds.

Sample scenario #1: Steve says to Tim, his direct report, "Hey, Tim, can you get these engineering specs for the Acme project done by Friday at noon?" "Sure, no worries," says Tim. By the time Steve gets around to opening the file at 4:45 on Friday afternoon, he is horrified to see that Tim's view of the project, the scope of the specs needed, and the level of detail are all too casual. "Rats," Steve mumbles to himself, "I may have to write that guy up."

Sample scenario #2: Gabriela makes it a point to celebrate everyone's birthday on her team. Cake in the lunchroom, shiny balloons, and a card that everyone signs are always part of the package. She hires Emily and notes that Emily's birthday occurs in two weeks, so Gabriela sets the standard procedure into place, knowing that this will help Emily feel welcome. When Emily arrives at work that morning, she sees all the party

stuff and runs out of the office in tears. Gabriela later finds out that Emily's mother died on her birthday last year (and it just so happens that Emily is diabetic and can't eat the cake anyway).

Why will this help me at work? Without clear expectations, shared assumptions, and defined commitments, we often get confused about where work is at, where it's going, and who's responsible for what. Add satellite locations, language, ethnic cultures, departmental subcultures, and generational differences, just to name a few, and you've got a lot of possibilities for misunderstanding.

Why is this so difficult at times? First, we cannot (nor should we) check and challenge every assumption. Second, understanding is different from agreement—too often we start to defend our position or logic before we have truly listened to the other. Third, it sometimes feels like it takes more time to be clear about our communication, so we're tempted to just plunge ahead and clean up any potential mess later.

Your frank self-assessment:
- How many times in the last ninety days have you been puzzled about why some communication with a team member went *thud*? Can you examine what your contributions might have been to not being clear?
- Do you have a tendency to carefully construct your logical reasons why people should shift their perspective, and then find yourself frustrated or disappointed when they didn't?
- When is the last time you asked for feedback about your patterns of making assumptions or not being clear in your expectations?

Flip's tips:
- There is an alternative to always chasing people down to get what you need. Don't participate in either sending or receiving "squishy" language (like "I'll try …," or "Sure, I'll look into it"). Bring focused awareness to making sure that commitments are stated clearly in terms of task, time line, ownership, and responsible party.
- When in doubt, ask (without a negative edge, please). Sometimes we are genuinely surprised as to how someone else can have a completely different interpretation of what we thought was a basic shared concept.
- To stay lighthearted, be on the lookout for humorous examples of misunderstandings. When I worked for a European company, they

sent over a batch of marketing materials that were all printed with the slogan, "We put the ordinary into the extraordinary." After we had a good laugh, we proceeded to design our own.

Action for traction:
- Find a friendly colleague and ask him or her to rate you on the following qualities: capability to deliver clear expectations, ability to be curious about shared definitions, giving and getting firm commitments.
- What are the biggest unclear mutual concepts or language for you or your team at work? Often these fall into clichés like: deliverables, quality service, prompt action, strategic planning, and so on. Make a list, and work through them to create specifics.
- Remember that relying too much on either intellect or emotion seldom brings others along with us. Too much emotional heat, and often others argue or withdraw—not enough, and it is a dry discourse.

Baked-in benefits:
- A commitment to continuous improvement in this area means that we assume positive intent when we hit a snag, and therefore we open up the conversation, rather than close it down.
- Being curious rather than judgmental ("Help me understand …") reduces tension and disconnection.
- Enhancing the skill of active listening produces better outcomes and stronger relationships.

For a deeper dive …
Ford, Jeffrey, and Laurie Ford. *The Four Conversations: Daily Communications That Gets Results.* Oakland, CA: Berrett-Koehler Publishers, 2009.

Gorman, Carol Kinsey. *The Non-Verbal Advantage: Secrets and Science of Body Language at Work.* Oakland, CA: Berrett-Koehler Publishers, 2008.

… and on the Web:
Adams, Susan. "How to Communicate Effectively at Work." *Forbes Magazine.* November 19, 2013. Accessed August 2, 2014. http://www.forbes.com/sites/susanadams/2013/11/19/how-to-communicate-effectively-at-work-3/

Mind Tools. "How Good Are Your Communication Skills? Speaking, Listening, Writing, and Reading Effectively." Accessed August 2, 2014. http://www.mindtools.com/pages/article/newCS_99.htm

NOTES AND NOODLINGS

CHAPTER 8

We'd Have a Wonderful Relationship If It Weren't for You—The Temptation to Blame

> "When you blame and criticize others, you are
> avoiding some truth about yourself."
> —DEEPAK CHOPRA

What it is … When we experience discomfort or disconnect in a relationship, one of our first tendencies is to find fault with the other, to view him in a negative light, and to express these thoughts and feelings to those around us.

Sample scenario #1: Oscar finds his supervisor to be challenging to work with. In Oscar's opinion, Bob is inconsistent in his focus, feedback, and praise. Instead of Oscar initiating a conversation with Bob, he often has lunch with Orville, and they spend much of the time denigrating Bob, his quirks, and his perceived performance deficiencies. Coworkers steer clear of them during breaks, and Oscar is puzzled why others don't see Bob's weaknesses as clearly as he does.

Sample scenario #2: When Betty is in meetings with Sally, she is uncomfortable with what she has determined to be Sally's brownnosing—speaking directly to the boss without making eye contact with others, for example. Betty makes snide comments to the person next to her—not loud enough for Sally to hear—about the "golden child," and as the meeting ends, Betty says to Frank, "Did you see how she was batting her eyes at him?" Betty is in search of someone who will triangulate.

Why will this help me at work? When we blame others, a multitude of unhelpful consequences occur. First, it does not move us any closer to identifying and solving business or relationship problems. Second, it invites

others to blame us, and lastly, it creates an unhealthy culture that impacts trust.

Why is this so difficult at times? In one sense blaming others "works"—in that it is a way, albeit a dysfunctional one, to discharge our feelings of disappointment or frustration. In addition, many of us come from families where this was so much the norm that it was invisible in either blatant or subtle ways. Much of today's political discourse is almost completely based on finding fault and assigning blame (instead of taking responsibility for what can be changed), and much of our media takes this same approach.

Your frank self-assessment:
- Who are the "incompetents" whom you work with? Make up a full list. Are you surprised at who they are or how many are on the list?
- What feels good about targeting others? As difficult as it might be to admit, jot down the ways.
- What are the conditions that are most likely to generate a blaming response on your part? Can you figure out the role stress plays in wanting to "let someone have it?"

Flip's tips:
- Consider the tendency to assign fault and blame as a sign of the need to develop your emotional intelligence more fully.
- Shift to a practice of empathy—this is the universal antidote to distancing ourselves from others by finding fault in them.
- Remember that sometimes we get "triggered" by someone at work because she represents unresolved dynamics from our past.

Action for traction:
- Find someone at work who doesn't seem to get his buttons pushed by the people who push yours, and invite him to have lunch or a cup of coffee. Ask how he is able to keep a "Zen approach" in interactions with these folks.
- Shift to the "observer" role—imagine yourself as a movie camera, simply recording all of the interactions at work without judgment. Look for places to "rise above."
- Invite one of your trusted colleagues to engage in a little role play, and have her give you helpful feedback first, then get her to shift to "it's your fault." Notice how it feels to be the recipient.

Baked-in benefits:
- You'll release emotional energy and blocks of time that will help you to be more productive.
- You'll take less negativity home with you.
- Your coworkers will take more delight in being around you!

For a deeper dive …
Alasko, Carl. *Beyond Blame: Freeing Yourself from the Most Toxic Form of Emotional Bulls**t*. New York: Tarcher, 2011.

Kotter, Jeffrey A. *Beyond Blame: A New Way of Resolving Conflicts in Relationships*. Hoboken, NJ: Jossey-Bass, 1996.

… and on the Web:
Ashoka. "Empathy in Business: Indulgence or Invaluable?" *Forbes Magazine*. March 23, 2013. Accessed August 2, 2014. http://www.forbes.com/sites/ashoka/2013/03/22/empathy-in-business-indulgence-or-invaluable/

McKay, Dawn Rosenberg. "The Five Difficult People You Meet at Work." About: Career Planning. Accessed August 2, 2014. http://careerplanning.about.com/od/bosscoworkers/a/difficultpeople.htm

NOTES AND NOODLINGS

CHAPTER 9

A Middle Path between Avoidance and Aggressiveness—The Art of Supportive Confrontation

"What we have to confront in the present workplace is the reluctance to engage in conversations that really invite the creative qualities hidden deep inside each human being."
—DAVID WHYTE

What it is … I don't know about you, but my old approach to conflict only had three options: (1) be really, really nice and hope things would get better, (2) run like hell (literally or internally) from the situation, or (3) get tired of holding that beach ball under the water and let them have it! What I didn't know at the time is that there is a specific set of skills for both dealing with the issue and staying positive in relationships. Supportive confrontation is being in service of the principle or standard at hand, while being both courageous and compassionate.

Sample scenario #1: Betsy has the same experience at the staff meeting every week—George will inevitably interrupt her. She puts on a good face, but inside she is secretly fuming. She can fantasize several ways to "put him in his place," but of course she knows that this will make things worse. Betsy thinks about carefully composing an e-mail to ask George to stop interrupting her, but she knows how easily tone can be misread in an e-mail, and it becomes part of the company record. She doesn't know what to do.

Sample scenario #2: Chen is a new employee with tons of ideas—and some of them are good ones. However, he frequently interjects them without much sensitivity to the agenda, the practicality, or the impact. Angela, his supervisor, tells him that (1) she appreciates his energy and drive, (2) she invites him to understand the unintended impact of his spontaneous

insertions, and (3) she will work will him on a regular basis to increase his awareness and to take responsibility for regulating his contributions.

Why will this help me at work? Getting a reasonable understanding and then demonstrating reasonable competency of this skill can be one of the most powerful tools for change, team alignment, and personal satisfaction. If we can move out of blaming (and its close cousin, triangulation), negativity, and ineffectiveness in having the conversations we need to have, then a great deal of untapped potential can be released for us and our teams.

Why is this so difficult at times? This is easy to answer—virtually none of us got any good training or modeling on the specifics of how to do this (I know I sure didn't!). We hold back on initiating the challenging conversation for a number of reasons—we don't want to be the cause of negative feelings in the other, we are uncertain about how to frame the dialogue and move through it, we are nervous about the outcome, and so on. This model takes practice (and often a coach) to implement well over time. It's not quick or easy, but it is accessible and immensely valuable.

Your frank self-assessment:
- What's your Conflict Avoidance Score (CAS)? (Hint: I just made up the CAS, so use whatever method you want as long as it's honest!)
- How much is your emotional reactivity a factor in your inability to discuss what matters?
- What happens internally for you when you can't "hold your center" during a conversation that has some heat?

Flip's tips:
- The root of the word "courage" is the French word "*coeur*," which means "heart." Make your courageous conversations heart-filled.
- Keep in mind that when our frustration boils over, we give the other person the perfect "evidence" that we are in fact the problem.
- Think about a specific time where you have grown because someone gave you information that you initially didn't want to hear.

Action for traction:
- Find someone who you think moves through difficult situations well. Ask him if you can interview him (better yet, buy lunch) and take the reporter's stance on gleaning information.
- Ask one of your closest associates if you can practice giving each other feedback—real or imagined—that would be challenging to give or receive. Choose doing this in a safe setting to start.

- Draw up a list of the qualities that you want to bring to your interactions with others, no matter how smooth or rough they may be. Where do you need to upgrade your competencies?

Baked-in benefits:
- I can almost guarantee that you'll experience less stress, for sure!
- After some practice, you should have more efficiency in your daily efforts.
- When we do this reasonably well, it deepens our connections.

For a deeper dive ...
Patterson, Kerry, Joseph Grenny, Ron McMillan, and Al Switzler. *Crucial Conversations: Tools for Talking When the Stakes Are High.* 2nd ed. New York: McGraw-Hill, 2011.

Scott, Susan. *Fierce Conversations: Achieving Success at Work and In Life One Conversation at a Time.* New York: Berkley Trade, 2004.

Stone, Douglas, Bruce Patton, and Sheila Heen. *Difficult Conversations: How to Discuss What Matters Most.* rev. ed. New York: Penguin, 2010.

... and on the Web:
CEDR. *"How to Handle Conflict and Confrontation: Keys to Managing, Resolving, and Working Through Disagreements*—National Seminars Training. http://www.nationalseminarstraining.com/events/events.cfm?tc=YHTMC

"Employee Confrontation Techniques for the Conflict Avoidant." Accessed August 2, 2014. http://www.cedrsolutions.com/employee-confrontation-techniques//

Myatt, Mike. "5 Ways of Dealing with Workplace Conflict." *Forbes.* February 22, 2012. Accessed August 2, 2014. http://www.forbes.com/sites/mikemyatt/2012/02/22/5-keys-to-dealing-with-workplace-conflict/

NOTES AND NOODLINGS

SECTION FOUR

Self-at-Work—Tools Are Good, but Just Having a Nice Set of Screwdrivers Won't Cut It

CHAPTER 10

A Seesaw of Effectiveness—
Balancing Tasks and Relationships

*"The simple act of paying positive attention to people
has a great deal to do with productivity."*
—TOM PETERS

What it is ... While there is a premium placed on task management in virtually all workplace settings, we cannot achieve optimal results without effective relationships across the organization. Knowing when, where, and how to shift our energies on this continuum can be a valuable component to our success.

Sample scenario #1: Mateo is the Finance Manager, and no one can crank out a spreadsheet like he can. He is the master of data, the king of analyses, and the prince of projections. His primary challenge is that he believes there is little value in conversations about anything other than the nuts and bolts of the business. Consequently, his colleagues tend to craft work-arounds instead of dealing with him directly, and his output suffers accordingly.

Sample scenario #2: Imani is keenly on top of how everyone is doing and how they are feeling. At the weekly staff meeting, she leads a check-in and encourages others to share freely about what's going on at work and in their personal lives to the extent that they're comfortable. She misses the cues that some employees are reluctant to open up, chalking that up as "shyness." Meanwhile, the agenda is hastily put together and seldom addressed thoroughly.

Why will this help me at work? Having the awareness and capability to make conscious changes—sometimes focusing more on task accomplishment, other times investing in effective business relationships—is a means to have more balance and better results.

Why is this so difficult at times? There are a number of challenges in this area. Our personal wiring may be such that we are on one end of this continuum or another. Stereotypically in this culture, men are supported to focus on tasks rather than relationships, and women get the opposite message from time to time. There are certain professions that attract those who resonate with one or the other style—engineering, finance, and IT professionals tend toward the task-management category, while the helping professions like nursing, education, and counseling have more of a relational focus.

Your frank self-assessment:
- Where is your comfort zone? Do you love being in "processing conversations" with others, or do you like to focus more on a concrete project?
- When and how do you consciously shift gears when you realize that your normal style is not particularly useful in a given situation?
- What do others think about your ability to utilize your strengths along with compensating for your difficulties in this area?

Flip's tips:
- Watch how moving toward your opposite competency usually spikes some anxiety, because it takes us into unknown territory.
- Notice that "control freak" and "touchy-feely" are the negative terms associated with these styles of being primarily task-focused or relationship-oriented. Think about the strengths that come along with them as well.
- Work on developing your awareness in the moment (like many of the other concepts discussed in this book) of where you might need to make a mindful shift between focusing on tasks versus relationships.

Action for traction:
- Find a self-assessment tool like the "FYI"—a system from Lominger—and pick out your strengths and challenges around task and relationship management. Choose three things you're good at and three you want to improve.
- Initiate a conversation with a work group you have good trust with—do they see you (and do you see them) as needing to broaden any competencies in this area? Schedule a follow-up.
- Who do you know and respect who could coach you on your weak side? Ask them if you can buy them a cup of their favorite beverage to gain their perspective.

Baked-in benefits:
- You'll be more of a "utility player"—taskmaster when it's needed, key connector at other times.
- Demonstrated flexibility in this area means that you can manage your stress better because you have more options.
- It's just more fun rather than being locked into only one perspective!

For a deeper dive ...
Reina, Dennis S., and Michelle L. Reina. *Trust and Betrayal in the Workplace: Building Effective Relationships in Your Organization.* 2nd ed. Oakland, CA: Berrett-Koehler Publishers, 2006.

Schmidt, Terry. *Strategic Project Management Made Simple: Practical Tools for Leaders and Teams.* Hoboken, NJ: Wiley, 2009.

... and on the Web:
Rosenblatt, Gideon. "Balancing Tasks and Relationships—The Art of Engagement." *Alchemy of Change Blog.* November 2, 2010. Accessed August 2, 2014. http://www.alchemyofchange.net/the-art-of-engagement/

Rykrsmith, Eva. "The Leadership Balancing Act: Results-Oriented vs. People-Oriented." *The Fast Track.* February 7, 2014. http://quickbase.intuit.com/blog/2014/02/07/the-leadership-balancing-act-results-oriented-vs-people-oriented//

Rykrsmith, Eva. "Team Troubleshooting: Balancing Tasks and People." *The Fast Track.* March 9, 2010. Accessed August 2, 2014. http://quickbase.intuit.com/blog/2010/03/09/team-troubleshooting-balancing-tasks-and-people/

NOTES AND NOODLINGS

CHAPTER 11

Clear, Useful Power—The Difference between Authoritative and Authoritarian

"The most common way people give up their
power is by thinking they don't have any."
—ALICE WALKER

What it is … Yes, I was one of those starry-eyed individuals (OK, technically a "hippie") who thought that if we could just get the right crew of groovy people together, things would work out somehow. Well, that got me/us a certain distance, but nowhere near far enough. There are times and places where we do need to exercise appropriate power—on the personal, professional, and organizational levels—not to use it over people, or as a mask for our own insecurity, but as a means of respectful service.

Sample scenario #1: The Acme Esoteric Supply Company has weekly meetings, where all business decisions of any minor significance are put on the agenda to be determined by virtue of full consensus. Unfortunately, some team members are growing more frustrated because additional items are added every week without resolving the issues already on the list since no consensus means no decision.

Sample scenario #2: Fritz believes he is benevolent in his authority and tries to take in everyone's point of view. The thing that drives his team nuts is that he often has to make a decision and waffles on it because he knows he can't please everyone, so he ends up pleasing no one because of this inaction.

Why will this help me at work? Everyone has some element of power in his or her position, regardless of rank or experience (assuming it's owned and practiced reasonably well). How we take a clear stance, how we take

care of ourselves, and how we advocate for what feels right and just are all additional ways that we can be of service to the enterprise.

Why is this so difficult at times? The primary reluctance to own or exercise authority is based on two underlying fears. The first is "If I challenge those who have more perceived power than me, I will potentially suffer negative consequences," including the dreaded "termination." On the other hand, for those who have power by virtue of defined position, the concern is "by exercising that power, I won't be liked."

Your frank self-assessment:
- Are you one of those who "chafe at authority," whether it belongs to you or others?
- Where in your life do you feel like you have a sense of your balanced personal power (it could even be at a bowling alley!)?
- What keeps you from taking risks when you need to challenge someone who you believe has more power or authority than you?

Flip's tips:
- Think about the wordplay between "authoritarian" and "authoritative"—one is about imposing, while the other is about disclosing, proposing, and then making it happen.
- You may want to check and see if there are some "old ghosts" in terms of bad authorities. (For me it was Mrs. Rice with that dreaded wooden paddle in fifth grade.) Be aware of when those old reactions may appear now.
- Reframe the negative feelings of someone having more authority over you. Move toward a place where others are in the midst of similar struggles in terms of how to be both a businessperson and a human being.

Action for traction:
- Make a list of your "ordinary powers" and your "superpowers"—if you don't believe you have any (or enough), ask a trusted advisor.
- Imagine yourself as the Queen or King of your workplace. What would you do differently? What capacities would you need to look at and change so that you could be both caring and accomplished?
- Write down some areas where you want more power or authority (or even less).

Baked-in benefits:
- It's wonderful to have less fault, blame, and fear when we deal with those in power.
- You actually can experience a greater ease at being yourself regardless of who's in the room.
- One real outcome can be the option of growing your sphere of influence.

For a deeper dive ...
Greenleaf, Robert K. *The Power of Servant Leadership.* Oakland, CA: Berrett-Koehler Publishers, 1998.

Sommer, Linda. *Beyond Office Politics: The Hidden Story of Power, Affiliation, and Achievement in the Workplace.* Charleston, SC: CreateSpace Independent Publishing Platform, 2012.

... and on the Web:
LaBier, Douglas. "How Does Having Power Over Others at Work Affect You?" *Psychology Today.* April 14, 2013. Accessed August 2, 2014. http://www.psychologytoday.com/blog/the-new-resilience/201304/how-does-having-power-over-others-work-affect-you

Lauby, Sharlyn. "The 7 Kinds of Power You Can Use at Work." *HR Bartender.* December 22, 2013. Accessed August 2, 2014. http://www.hrbartenderbetter-leadership.com/2013/recruiting/the-7-kinds-of-power-you-can-use-at-work//

NOTES AND NOODLINGS

CHAPTER 12

How to Achieve More by Engaging Less (Or, "Boundaries R Me")

"'No' is a complete sentence."
—ANNE LAMOTT

What it is ... Setting clear boundaries and limits is an important component of managing both our work and our stress. Sometimes boundaries are firm; sometimes they're flexible—but if they're unclear, inconsistent, or nonexistent, it doesn't serve us well or those around us.

Sample scenario #1: Kayla is a helper. She helps her teammates, members of other teams, a host of volunteer organizations, and oh yes, her family. She frequently is engaged from 6:00 a.m. to 10:00 p.m. What few suspect is that Kayla feels at risk of a total collapse.

Sample scenario #2: Matt's challenge is that he loves to socialize with his coworkers, and is the first to say, "I'll buy you one." He went out for a few drinks with his manager's administrative assistant, which led to dinner, then dancing, then a blurry memory of going too far. Now his career is in jeopardy.

Why will this help me at work? The ability to set flexible and reasonable limits helps make sure that job descriptions don't become runaway trains, that time and energy are more balanced, and that we have clarity in our relationships.

Why is this so difficult at times? Several factors enter—fear that others will misunderstand our need or request, that we don't actually have the capability in the system to set limits, or that we will be judged as not being a "team player" if we don't take anything and everything that's thrown at us.

Your frank self-assessment:
- What happens when you try to graciously say (or accept) the word "no"?
- Do you wish you weren't so overcommitted? If so, where can you "prune your tree" so that you get better "fruit"? (So you don't drive yourself nuts, remember?)
- When you think about declining an invitation from someone you care about to take on another task, what feelings are stirred up? How do you make sense of this emotional response? Does it serve you or constrain you?

Flip's tips:
- Identify places in your schedule that do not produce any value, and decide what you'll do next about these "time sponges."
- Examine any myths you may be holding about "if I don't do it, it's not going to get done well, on time, or at all."
- Check to see if you've got any family history that is relevant.

Action for traction:
- Start small—find one low-energy or low-return commitment that you can gracefully resign from.
- If you think people may believe that they will be negatively impacted by your choices, be proactive in letting them know that by taking care of yourself in this way, you're actually taking care of the relationship.
- Try to book an hour a week (for starters) where you put "Nothing" in your calendar—perhaps secretly—and then use that time to do whatever you feel you need when that time arises.

Baked-in benefits:
- You'll have more choices about how to apply your talents and energies.
- Over time, others will notice and respect your clarity and firmness.
- You will be providing excellent modeling for others.

For a deeper dive ...
Cloud, Henry. *Boundaries for Leaders: Results, Relationships, and Being Ridiculously in Charge.* New York: HarperBusiness, 2013.

Smith, Manuel J. *When I Say "No" I Feel Guilty.* New York: Bantam, 1985.

... and on the Web:
"The Benefits of Saying No." LinkedIn. April 8, 2014. Accessed August 2, 2014. https://www.linkedin.com/today/post/article/20140408170542 -10626019-the-benefits-of-saying-no

Chua, Celestine. "7 Simple Ways to Say No." *Zen Habits Blog.* August 3, 2010. Accessed August 2, 2014. http://zenhabits.net/say-no/

Gronlund, Christopher. "When and How to Say No." *Success Magazine.* http://www.success.com/article/when-and-how-to-say-no

NOTES AND NOODLINGS

SECTION FIVE

Self-in-Organizational-
Life—Why Are All of Us
Crazier Than Any of Us?

CHAPTER 13

Workplace as Yogurt—Chock-Full of Active Cultures

"Culture eats strategy for lunch."
—PETER DRUCKER

What it is … One definition of workplace culture is "a set of basic assumptions that defines for us what to pay attention to, what things mean, how to react emotionally to what is going on, and what actions to take in various kinds of situations" (Edgar Schein, *Organizational Culture and Leadership,* 4th ed., 2010:29). When we enter an organization, some of these basic assumptions are visible (differences in dress, whether phones are shut off during meetings) and others operate more invisibly (two key persons don't speak directly to each other because of an unresolved conflict, you're expected to take work home).

Sample scenario #1: Nathan moves from one company location to the other, and much to his surprise, the new plant is run much differently. He is told to "watch your back," that "you'll learn your place in the pecking order," and "if you need help understanding whose butt to kiss, just let me know." The thing that puzzles Nathan is that the plant's productivity is greater than the one he just left.

Sample scenario #2: Lucy was the administrative assistant to the founder of the company. For over thirty years she has been a dedicated employee, although her computer skills have not kept pace, her office looks like a paper tornado passed through, and she seems to come and go as she pleases. The new HR manager is on a mission to improve accountability throughout the organization; however, she is told to "give Lucy a pass."

Why will this help me at work? If you're not aware of the underlying assumptions of the culture you're working in, you may find that things

happen that just don't seem to make sense to you (e.g., promotions based on how much you work, not the quality of your work). Being able to delineate cultural attributes is the first step in changing them.

Why is this so difficult at times? Edgar Schein talks about how the longer someone has been in a particular organization, the harder it is for her to see the patterns of assumptions and behaviors—like asking the fish to describe the water. There are so many components to culture that it becomes important to focus on the elements that we want to bring into awareness and change, and there will be very different opinions and experiences around this.

Your frank self-assessment:
- Think of where you work as if it were a country or a state—what elements make it different from where you've lived before?
- What are some of the things that delight you or drive you crazy for lack of a rational explanation?
- If you were truly and totally in charge, what would be the first three patterns that you would change?

Flip's tips:
- Keep in mind that there is no ideal or perfect culture. What adds real value for one environment may not be optimal for another.
- If you've genuinely tried to "make work work" and it just isn't happening, maybe it's time to come to the conclusion that a given organizational culture is not a match. I truly valued the six years I spent in a large nonprofit, but in the end it was just too painfully slow to initiate and implement new business development for the way I wanted to work, so I moved on.
- It can be helpful to examine the biases we hold about both workplace and national cultures. Working for a European company for three years certainly taught me a lot about their food, wine, and art, but their workplace culture was fundamentally different in ways I hadn't anticipated.

Action for traction:
- If you work in an organization with more than one department, see if you can benevolently pick out some of the similarities and differences in the operational assumptions. For example, does one group have a "jeans Friday" while the other doesn't? Is there a

tendency to vote on decisions when consensus is taking too long, or is it deferred to the person in charge?
- Think about what a cultural assessment of your group would look like. Do you think you could do that on your own, or would it take someone from the outside with an independent stance?
- Design a strategic planning session, taking into account the optimal design, methodology, and outcomes that will serve you best.

Baked-in benefits:
- You'll have more tools to understand the complexities of work.
- There will be a clearer sense of how you fit (or not).
- You'll be able to initiate dialogues that serve a larger purpose.

For a deeper dive ...
Schein, Edgar H. *The Corporate Culture Survival Guide.* rev. ed. Hoboken, NJ: Jossey-Bass, 2009.

Schein, Edgar H. *Organizational Culture and Leadership.* 4th ed. Hoboken, NJ: Jossey-Bass, 2010.

... and on the Web:
Kotter, John. "The Key to Changing Organizational Culture." *Forbes.* September 27, 2012. Accessed August 2, 2014. http://www.forbes.com/sites/johnkotter/2012/09/27/the-key-to-changing-organizational-culture/

Margolis, Sheila. "Define Organizational Culture—and Why Should We Care?" *HBR Blog Network.* May 15, 2013. Accessed August 2, 2014. http://blogs.hbr.org/2013/05/what-is-organizational-culture/

Schein, Edgar H. "Coming to a New Awareness of Organizational Culture." *Sloan Management Review* 25, no. 2 (Winter 1984). IT Universe of Copenhagen. Accessed August 2, 2014. https://blog.itu.dk/SFOL-F2013/files/2013/03/culture_schein.pdf

NOTES AND NOODLINGS

CHAPTER 14

Bureaucracy, B.S., and Other Barriers—How to Deal with Unnecessary Energy Drains

"Simple, clear purpose and principles give rise to complex and intelligent behavior. Complex rules and regulations give rise to simple and stupid behavior."
—DEE HOCK

What it is ... We usually get so hung up on what we're supposed to be doing in organizations because—somewhat understandably—we do need to produce results. However, this causes our competencies in *how* things are decided and communicated to be much less robust. Thus, we fall back on protocols and procedures that reduce the creative energies around us.

Sample scenario #1: Darius has hired a talented administrative assistant who is getting her college degree by studying nights and weekends. She is bright, organized, dedicated, and appropriately ambitious. Her compensation has not been raised since she began working eighteen months ago, and documentation supports that she is working two to three pay grades above her starting point. Darius puts in for a two-level hourly wage increase, and his supervisor feels it is justified. Once his supervisor's boss's administrative assistant finds out, she raises a major stink because it took her three years to advance one grade, and the proposal stalls. After four months of negotiations, the increase is approved, but by then the talented young woman has given her notice.

Sample scenario #2: It has become apparent that one or two employees may have made repeated personal cell phone calls from the company restrooms during work time. Rather than speaking to these individuals, a new policy is instituted where bathroom breaks are limited to five minutes or less, unless the supervisor is notified in advance of "unusual circumstances." Negative chatter and "black humor" arise among staff.

Why will this help me at work? While you may often feel powerless to affect changes in policies and procedures, everyone can find a voice in recommending commonsense solutions. The challenge is to not get caught up in power struggles, blaming, or taking sides.

Why is this so difficult at times? This is the subject of many a Dilbert© cartoon. What seemingly start out as Standard Operating Procedures (SOPs) often turn into a maze of illogical and impractical dictates. The other factors include the openness of the leaders, managers, and culture to examine what is working and useful versus what is historical and obfuscated.

Your frank self-assessment:
- Are there places where you can improve your work processes, regardless of whether or not you can get approval?
- Do you take an active or passive approach to what's not working well?
- Are you able to stay curious rather than judgmental, and keep the harsh edge of resentment out of the dialogue?

Flip's tips:
- Ask yourself if the level of confusion, arbitrary rules, and inflexibility in your workplace are a "match" for you (after putting in good energy to change things). If they aren't, this generally means you should find a new professional home.
- Develop the skill of only presenting problems when you can also offer reasonable solutions, or at least first steps.
- "Dance lightly" (which is another way of saying "don't sweat the small stuff")—it can keep you from being bogged down in discouragement.

Action for traction:
- Make a "Top Ten" list of your bureaucratic frustrations in the system. Put a star next to the ones that you think you could find a way to initiate a helpful conversation about with someone in the organization.
- If you feel you can do so and it's appropriate for your position, take $40 out of your compensation and sponsor a contest where the top three suggestions for streamlining operational results get a $25, $10, and $5 music download gift card.

- Use your business relational skills to take a risk and challenge a leader with the goal of making this person more successful by eliminating a stinky corporate manure pile.

Baked-in benefits:
- You'll feel better if you don't give in to cynicism, but offer solutions.
- Perhaps you'll even be seen as a "change agent" (although some agents do come to harm, so be careful!).
- If a positive vibe becomes infectious, then whole teams can actually get on the bandwagon.

For a deeper dive …
Ackoff, Russell Lincoln, and Sheldon Rovin. *Beating the System: Using Creativity to Outsmart Bureaucracies.* Oakland, CA: Berrett-Koehler Publishers, 2005.

Dickson, Paul. *The Official Rules: 5,427 Laws, Principles, and Axioms to Help You Cope with Crises, Deadlines, Bad Luck, Rude Behavior, Red Tape, and Attacks by Inanimate Objects.* Mineola, NY: Dover, 2013.

… and on the Web:
Augustine, Avery. "How to Deal with the Worst Organizational Bureaucracy." The Muse. February 24, 2014. Accessed August 2, 2014. https://www.themuse.com/advice/how-to-deal-with-the-worst-organizational-bureaucracy

Babauta, Leo. "10 Steps to Take Action and Eliminate Bureaucracy." *Zen Habits.* November 16, 2008. Accessed August 2, 2014. http://zenhabits.net/10-steps-to-take-action-and-eliminate-bureaucracy/

The Good Project. "The Good Work Project Toolkit." Harvard Graduate School of Education. Accessed August 2, 2014. http://www.thegoodproject.org/good-work/the-good-work-project/the-goodwork-toolkit//

NOTES AND NOODLINGS

CHAPTER 15

Cluster Pluck—Finding the Courage and Tools to Get Better Outcomes in Group Settings

"If you had to identify, in one word, the reason why the human race has not achieved, and never will achieve, its full potential, that word would be 'meetings.'"
—DAVE BARRY

What it is ... Something seems to happen when we get together as a group or team in the workplace. It's like some invisible set of rules takes over (which, in fact, it often does). Having good in-the-moment awareness and a functional set of tools for understanding and working effectively as a collaborative group can be invaluable.

Sample scenario #1: Emily dreads the Wednesday staff meeting. Oliver is bound to brag about his weekend exploits before things get going, Hannah will bring a bunch of sugary baked goods to pass around, and Henry will always be playing *Angry Birds* under the table the whole time. Just once she'd like to tell people what she thinks of their behavior. Meanwhile, she makes shopping lists on her notepad.

Sample scenario #2: Jacob tries to have good relations with his cubby neighbors. He does his best to keep up on their birthdays, family changes, and other life events. He seems puzzled when he doesn't get cooperation from his team when he wants to organize after-work bowling parties and poker tournaments.

Why will this help me at work? Unless you truly work solo all day long (tempting, I know), you'll have to interact in group settings. Most of us rely on our personalities, which are necessary, but not sufficient. Being able to specify which decision-making model you'll be using, having an empathic way of dealing with unhelpful interruptions, and bringing awareness about

how your team has a low risk tolerance can help you increase your results and your satisfaction.

Why is this so difficult at times? Most of us received our "training" around the family dinner table, in terms of power, interactive conversations (or not), and decision making. Add to that the fear of speaking up given the risk that the "boss" just might judge you as not being smart enough or worthy enough, and it's enough to keep many of us from taking appropriate risks. Lastly, there's often someone who pushes our buttons, and without the practiced skill of supportive confrontation, we avoid starting a potential conflict (and mutter to ourselves or someone else).

Your frank self-assessment:
- What's your sense of being able to be both observer and participant in a group setting? Can you see what's happening with some degree of objectivity, instead of being "swept along"?
- How do you see yourself in terms of the ability to find the sweet spot between avoidance and aggressiveness? Are you able to "step into the conversation" when it is needed and appropriate?
- How do you define "team"? This is not as easy as it sounds. Once you have this, what roles are needed, and what is your current versus ideal responsibility?

Flip's tips:
- The trick is to get better at "process," not "content." Most groups (and meetings) focus almost exclusively on the subject matter of what they are organized to do, and not nearly enough on how they communicate, interact, resolve conflicts, and so on.
- White males need to be especially mindful that they have been culturally trained and supported—historically—to be the first to speak or to be heavy in the quantity of their contributions.
- Schedule breaks between meetings. It amazes me that the myth of the back-to-back sixty-minute appointment or meeting still exists in most workplaces. Since we all need a minimum of five minutes (ten is better) to hit the restroom, check e-mail, and get from point A to B, consecutive hour-long meetings inevitably set us up for being three to seven minutes late for the next one.

Action for traction:
- If you are the leader of a team or meeting, do some research on group norms, then facilitate a discussion on what you want to

consciously keep doing, what you want to stop doing, and what you want to add in terms of your process.

- Ask those you trust if they see any difference between your attributes and competencies on a one-on-one basis versus a group setting. If so, what shifts would be helpful for you to make?
- See if you can get your group to open up a different balance between knowing who's in the room on a personal basis as opposed to just professionally. Sometimes when we take the risk to share more of ourselves, it models appropriate vulnerability and acceptance.

Baked-in benefits:
- You'll get better outcomes in decisions, deadlines, and deliverables.
- There will be a more open, collaborative, and collegial atmosphere.
- You'll spend less time with negative thoughts and feelings.

For a deeper dive …
Levi, Daniel. *Group Dynamics for Teams.* 3rd ed. Thousand Oaks, CA: SAGE Publications, 2010.

Schein, Edgar H. *Humble Inquiry: The Gentle Art of Asking Instead of Telling.* Oakland, CA: Berrett-Koehler Publishers, 2013.

… and on the Web:
Brounstein, Marty. "Ten Qualities of an Effective Team Player." *Managing Teams For Dummies.* http://www.dummies.com/how-to/content/ten-qualities-of-an-effective-team-player.html

"How to Be a Good Team Player: Maximizing Your Contribution." Accessed August 2, 2014. http://www.mindtools.com/pages/article/newTMM_53.htm

HR Council Canada. "Workplaces That Work." Accessed August 2, 2014. http://hrcouncil.ca/hr-toolkit/workplaces-team-work.cfm

Sethi, Jappreet. "How to Build a Dream Team at Work." *Human Resources Blog.* 2014. http://www.humanresourcesblog.in/2014/06/03/how-to-build-a-dream-team-at-work/

NOTES AND NOODLINGS

SECTION SIX

Self-in-a-Larger-Sphere— Your Own Big Picture

CHAPTER 16

Don't Let Money Drive Your Boat ('Cause You'll End Up Sinking)

*"Money is like manure—when you spread it around,
it grows things. When you pile it up, it stinks."*
—UNKNOWN

What it is ... Our relationship with money is seldom one of ease. The popular myth is that managing abundance is far better than managing scarcity; however, they each have their own challenges and virtues. When our self-worth is too tightly tied to our compensation, bad things can happen, particularly when it comes time for the dreaded annual review. Money is a concentrated form of energy that we as humans made up, and we should keep in mind that it needs to be under our control, not the other way around.

Sample scenario #1: Scott is obsessed with how much he makes. He is frequently complaining about not getting a raise, about how the company must be raking in record profits, and that he deserves more than some of the "slackers" in the organization. He expects to be compensated more before he will do more, and works hard to not work an extra minute. Needless to say, Scott is not much fun to be around, nor does he get promoted.

Sample scenario #2: Julie is a great worker, a valued contributor, and an excellent team member. Her supervisor only has one complaint—Julie shops online on her paid lunch hour and on business trips. She is frequently heard complaining about her credit cards being maxed out, and has been known to ask other team members if they could "cover" the cost of her lunch orders as payday approaches.

Why will this help me at work? No one wants to be around someone who is financially needy, stressed out, or compulsive. Plus, many if not most

jobs require some knowledge of numbers, and some ability to be trusted around finances. If we are seen as primarily focused on our compensation, as opposed to our contributions, we can stifle our business relationships and advancement.

Why is this so difficult at times? Money almost always has strong emotional undercurrents associated with it. Growing up, we may have had the experience that money was invisible—it was liquid, it was painfully absent, it was tightly hoarded, or it was used as a reward system (to name a few). Interject that into our current cultural reality of big mortgages, upcoming college expenses, outstanding loans, the performance of our 401(k) plan, and future retirement needs, and there is plenty of potential stress to go around.

Your frank self-assessment:
- Have you been able to cruise through your varied financial situations with relative ease, or have you hit one pothole, detour, and crash after another?
- Google a list of all the available human emotions, and choose three positive emotions that you associate with finances, and three negative ones. How do these play out as you make your financial decisions?
- Are you realistic about where you are at and what your financial goals are, or do you specialize in deliberate denial?

Flip's tips:
- Rewrite your family history around money, changing the stories that were told and retold (implicitly and explicitly) around the meaning of money.
- Remember when, as a kid, you saved up for something special? Have you tried that lately? Articulate what it would mean to do so today.
- Imagine that a wizard appeared and said that you could have any nonmaterial thing in the world you wanted, but in order to do so, you would need to give up your ten most valued possessions. Make a list and see what it would feel like to let your precious things go.

Action for traction:
- Find someone whom you totally trust to get financially "naked" with (all your assets, debts, beautiful features, and warts exposed). Notice any feelings of pride, shame, anxiety, or fear.

- If overspending is your thing, leave your plastic—credit, debit, and ATM cards—and your checkbook at home for a week. See what happens when you run out of cash or you have to go to a physical bank to get cash. (Note: This is the only way our grandparents knew how to live!)
- Make a sheet with two columns. On one side, list all the things you do that you get paid for, and on the other write down the things you do that provide value in this world. Which is the larger list? What feelings arise?

Baked-in benefits:
- You'll be more at ease, and easier to be around.
- You'll be focused more on what's truly important.
- By being less stressed around money, you'll be in a better position to actually make more.

For a deeper dive …
Kinder, George. *The Seven Stages of Money Maturity: Understanding the Spirit and Value of Money in Your Life.* New York: Dell, 2000.

Twist, Lynne. *The Soul of Money: Reclaiming the Wealth of Our Inner Resources.* New York: W. W. Norton, 2006.

… and on the Web:
Millburn, Joshua Fields, and Ryan Nicodemus. *The Minimalists Blog.* Accessed August 2, 2014. http://www.theminimalists.com//

Slow Money Blog. June 13, 2014. Accessed August 2, 2014. https://slowmoney.org/blog/

Tasch, Woody. "The Slow Money Letter." Management. https://www.mint.com/

NOTES AND NOODLINGS

CHAPTER 17

Rockin' Your Roles—Balancing a 360-Degree View of All You Do

"Happiness is not a matter of intensity but of balance, order, rhythm, and harmony."
—THOMAS MERTON

What it is ... Balanced effectiveness at work is also related to and dependent upon how you move through the other areas of your life. Too often we experience competing needs, unclear priorities, and feelings of inadequacy. Our work roles and priorities need to fit into the larger realm of who we are and whom we love.

Sample scenario #1: Everyone marvels at Martina's energy. Not only does she put in fifty-hour weeks at work, she also is the coordinator for the community gardens near her home, writes a blog on quilting, and serves as an educator in her church. Oh, and did we mention that she has two teenagers to boot? Martina wishes she could get to a yoga class once in a while and spend more one-on-one time with her husband, but the pace goes on without a break, and Martina is sleeping less and less.

Sample scenario #2: Tom doesn't have the problem of doing too many things outside of work. His challenge is that every extra ounce of energy he has is spent on his commitment as a triathlete. From training logs to online research, from 6:00 a.m. pool swims to weekend marathons, he does two things—he works, and he trains. Meanwhile, friends and family are there to cheer him on when he competes, but see little of him otherwise. He feels as good as his last race result.

Why will this help me at work? Work requires energy, focus, and resiliency. All of these are tested when we try to serve the needs of others without

taking care of our own requirements, or conversely, only focus on ourselves. When we overcommit, we undervalue ourselves.

Why is this so difficult at times? We have internal messages that seem to say "people need you" or "they'll be disappointed if you say no" or "family comes first." We think spending time in solitude, or worse yet, "doing nothing" is selfish, so we go, go, go.

Your frank self-assessment:
- In one of your areas of responsibility, try to draw a continuum from "service" to "sacrifice" to "martyr." Where are you at your best and worst levels of engagement?
- What happens from a feelings standpoint when you look at giving up one of your roles?
- What have you been thinking about in terms of making better use of your precious time?

Flip's tips:
- Examine your primary focus—are you a "human doing" or a "human being"?
- Try not to bite off more than you can chew. Many high-performing individuals commit the "sin" of trying to provide too much value. They have helped in one area successfully, so why not several more? The result is that there is so much on their plates that they have forgotten what size, shape, or color it is!
- Know when to say "no." You may be like me and a lot of folks I work with, and be a "possibility junkie." Ooh, there are so many neat, cool, wonderful, and helpful things I could do in the world ... So, we say "yes" without thinking through the implications.

Action for traction:
- Write down all the roles that you currently own. How many do you actually have? Is the list scary, or is it interesting to write them all down? Ask those closest to you for their perspective.
- Take two or three areas of responsibility that you feel are most burdensome. Create a "job description" for each, and then see if there are components that can be delegated or "sold" to others.
- If there are things you have taken on that you really need to transition out of, find a trusted friend to help you write up an "exit strategy," with goals and time lines. Soon you'll be free!

Baked-in benefits:
- With better balance comes a better attitude.
- You'll actually get more done.
- You'll be more present for those you care about.

For a deeper dive …
Kelly, Matthew. *Off Balance: Getting Beyond the Work-Life Balance Myth to Personal and Professional Satisfaction.* New York: Hudson Street Press, 2011.

Merrill, Roger A., and Rebecca Merrill. *Life Matters: Creating a Dynamic Balance of Work, Family, Time, & Money.* New York: McGraw-Hill, 2004.

Whyte, David. *The Three Marriages: Reimagining the Relationship to Self, the Other, and Work.* New York: Riverhead, 2010.

… and on the Web:
Caprino, Kathy. "Ten Commitments of People Achieving Successful Work-Life Integration." *Forbes.* June 16, 2014. Accessed August 2, 2014. http://www.forbes.com/sites/kathycaprino/2014/06/16/10-commitments-of-people-achieving- successful-work-life-integration/

Duffy, Karl. *Tiny Buddha Blog.* Accessed August 2, 2014. http://tinybuddha.com/

Mindful Balance Blog. Accessed August 2, 2014. http://mindfulbalance.org//

NOTES AND NOODLINGS

CHAPTER 18

Compassionately Engaged, but Not Entangled— The Rewards of Healthy Detachment

"Once you stop being locked into viewing reality from just one perspective, you will start to be free from habitual reactivity."
—STEPHEN RICHARDS

What it is ... When we are whipsawed by our emotions, when we are fixated on a desired outcome, and when we simply need people to behave in the ways we need them to, we set ourselves up for frustration (not to mention impacting our results). The art of healthy detachment is not being aloof, uncaring, or disconnected—it is being attentive, connected, and caring, but without internal drama or the lack of being centered.

Sample scenario #1: Maggie is a nurse in the Emergency Department. She sees everything from a kid with a broken elbow to a car accident victim who dies on the table. When asked how she does this without being overwhelmed, Maggie talks about the concept of "emotional calluses"— the idea that you need a certain amount of "tough skin" to deal with the traumas and tragedies that are part of the job, but you can't be so insensitive as to lose your empathy and appropriate bedside manner.

Sample scenario #2: Aaron works in a call center, providing world-class customer service to a wide variety of individuals. They present with a full spectrum of emotionality—from grateful to frustrated to confused to angry. Regardless of whether the caller is positive, neutral, or negative, Aaron gives him all the same warmth and service. From time to time, he needs to set limits with the unreasonable; however, virtually everyone who calls him with a problem feels heard and understood.

Why will this help me at work? Being able to notice how our thoughts and emotions rise and fall, where and when we get triggered, and how

our buttons get pushed is an invaluable skill, regardless of position or industry. We've all been on the receiving end of someone's tirade, and it stops all constructive dialogue. When we can see the swirling currents of reactivity—theirs and ours—we have the option to choose our responses.

Why is this so difficult at times? This requires a high degree of consciousness on two levels—what is happening in terms of the observable behaviors and interactions in the moment, and the awareness of our own internal states. Much of the time when we get caught up in feeling attacked, wounded, denigrated, frustrated, or irritated, our emotional state takes over and drives the boat.

Your frank self-assessment:
- Think back to a recent time when you "lost it" (even if it didn't result in an outburst). What helpful information can you extract from this situation?
- Conversely, can you think of a time when you were the calm captain in the raging seas as the rest of the crew freaked out? What helped you keep your cool?
- Where is your leading edge of learning and practice in terms of reactivity?

Flip's tips:
- Consider adding some sort of mindfulness practice if you don't already have one. Not sure what to do? Ask around—you'll likely be surprised how many people you already know who quietly have one.
- Often, our reactivity is rooted in some historical origins. Do the hard work of figuring out those beginnings.
- When being assertive, take a clear, firm stance based on clarity rather than impulsiveness.

Action for traction:
- Design your own mini-360-degree feedback survey (online and anonymous, if you wish) to see how others view you in terms of your ability to move through work's challenges calmly.
- Think about a person or situation that is more likely to cause you to be reactive. Map out your options in advance.
- Find someone whom you experience as being rather unflappable. Buy her lunch and ask how she does it.

Baked-in benefits:
- You'll have a better experience moving through your workday.
- People around you will also have a better experience.
- This works well at home too!

For a deeper dive …
Carroll, Michael. *Awake at Work: 35 Practical Buddhist Principles for Discovering Clarity and Balance in the Midst of Work's Chaos.* Boston: Shambala, 2006.

Casey, Karen. *Let Go Now: Embracing Detachment.* Newburyport, MA: Conari Press, 2010.

… and on the Web:
Chaudhuri, Anita. "How I Stay Calm, by People With Very Stressful Jobs." *The Guardian.* February 28, 2014. Accessed August 2, 2014. http://www.theguardian.com/lifeandstyle/2014/mar/01/how-stay-calm -by-people-stressful-jobs

Tanjeloff, Jasmin. "How to Create a Balanced Life: 9 Tips to Feel Calm and Grounded." *Tiny Buddha.* Accessed•August 2, 2014. http://tinybuddha. com/blog/9-tips-to-create-a-balanced-life/

Zen Habits Blog. Accessed August 2, 2014. http://zenhabits.net/

NOTES AND NOODLINGS

SECTION SEVEN

Not-Self—Connecting with
Something Bigger Than
Your Singular Soul

CHAPTER 19

As Mr. Dylan Said, "You Gotta Serve Somebody"

"The best way to find yourself is to lose
yourself in the service of others."
—MAHATMA GANDHI

What it is ... When we're solely focused on chasing our own success, we run the risk of shutting ourselves off from the world around us, and fail to see how our talents are best used for something other than our exclusive gain. Being in service not only provides value to the recipient, but also helps us to "get out of our own way" and grow.

Sample scenario #1: John used to stop by his neighborhood bar most evenings after work, not sure what he was looking for or why he was there. His brother-in-law asked him to sub at the Boys and Girls Club, and John has found it much more rewarding than warming a barstool.

Sample scenario #2: Mei was asked to mentor a special-needs student at her daughter's school. At first she thought, *I have no time for this,* but has found that doing this volunteer work has actually enabled her to shift how she views time, since the young woman she is helping needs her full patience.

Why will this help me at work? Whatever the mix of service inside and outside of work, it almost always broadens our perspective and increases our compassion. Of course, one must take the same balanced approach to setting limits on our service work as with other elements in life. However, giving to others seldom has a downside.

Why is this so difficult at times? First, we get so caught up in our own personal dramas and perceived needs that we don't necessarily think to extend ourselves to others. Second, we may feel overwhelmed, since there is an endless list of needs where we could plug in. Lastly, we may temporarily forget the set of positive feelings that comes from helping others.

Your frank self-assessment:
- We can be of service formally (in a designated role) and informally (seeing a situation where we can be helpful). How do you apply your energies?
- Are any of your service efforts secretly designed or implemented with the hidden hope that you will gain stature, validation, or rewards from your efforts? If so, examine these internal dynamics, for others will pick them up at some point.
- Can you stretch yourself in terms of working with populations that are not at all like you?

Flip's tips:
- Identify your own categories of service, including (but not limited to) volunteering time to accomplish physical tasks, mentoring and coaching others, being on a nonprofit board, and making financial contributions. What other ones am I missing here?
- Make sure that you're clear about the expectations and parameters around your service work so that you're not harboring resentment later. I love the humor in "Doing work when you know you're not going to get paid is called 'pro bono.' Doing work thinking you're going to get paid and you don't is called 'amateur bono.'"
- Sometimes we have to allow ourselves to accept help in order to help others. Make sure you're not locked into a role that doesn't allow you to be vulnerable in the right time and place.

Action for traction:
- Make a list of the ways in which you provide service to others and the roles you play in doing so (routine or necessary obligations don't count for this exercise). Where are you overextended? Where would you like to increase your efforts?
- Start a brown-bag lunch series at work, inviting representatives from volunteer organizations to come in once a month to educate the folks in your workforce about what they do to make your community a better place and how you and your coworkers might plug in.
- Pick an organization whose values and mission you admire. Offer them ten hours of your time, energy, and talent with no strings and no expectations. When the project is done, engage in a mutual evaluation in terms of what you and your contact learned.

Baked-in benefits:
- You'll enrich your experience and that of others.
- You'll be contributing to a stronger community and a better world.
- You might even whine and complain less.

For a deeper dive …
Ausenda, Fabio. *Green Volunteers: The World Guide to Voluntary Work in Nature Conservations.* 8th ed. New York: Universe, 2011.

McMillon, Bill, Doug Cutchens, and Anne Geissinger. *Volunteer Vacations: Short-Term Adventures That Will Benefit You and Others.* 11th ed. Chicago: Chicago Review Press, 2012.

… and on the Web:
Action for Happiness. Accessed August 2, 2014. http://www.actionfor happiness.org/

Volunteer Match. Accessed August 2, 2014. http://www.volunteermatch.org/

NOTES AND NOODLINGS

CHAPTER 20

Your Mother Was Right When She Said, "Go Play Outside"—The Beneficial Effects of Being in Nature

"The best remedy for those who are afraid, lonely or unhappy is to go outside, somewhere where they can be quite alone with the heavens, nature and God."
—ANNE FRANK

What it is ... There is a natural rhythm to life that is not found in office buildings, malls, or homes. It is *especially* difficult to understand and feel this fundamental source of energy when we're plugged into our electronic devices 24/7. Being in nature puts us back in touch with how we got here, what sustains us, and our need to be mindful stewards of this lovely blue-and-green planet.

Sample scenario #1: As CEO, Samantha faces incredible pressure—increasing the company's earnings, driving new business development, keeping the workforce reasonably happy, dealing with changing markets and technology; it's a wonder she can sleep at night. However, each month there will always be one day on her calendar—sometimes planned well in advance, sometimes with just a few days' notice, when it's "Disappearance Day." This means that Samantha is outside—on a trail, in her kayak, or sliding down a mountain—because it is what she needs to do to stay refreshed and resilient.

Sample scenario #2: Dylan has three rigid rules when it comes to running his department—shut off the HVAC and open the windows when it makes sense to do so, don't wear socks if you don't want to, and your team can meet outside anytime it wants. He organizes events like giving his team a fixed budget and then challenging them to come up with the best lunch they can buy and assemble from the farmer's market. He insists that for each of the four seasons there be one strategic meeting off-site that involves

being in the fresh air, regardless of the weather at the time. His team loves him.

Why will this help me at work? Unless you are lucky enough to work outside, most of us are trapped in closed environments that often drain rather than sustain our energy. The natural world gives us both a respite and a source of inspiration to do our best.

Why is this so difficult at times? As creatures of habit, we can easily convince ourselves that all the "important" stuff leaves us no time or energy to get out and about. We may think that to truly spend time in nature requires a vacation (when it obviously doesn't), or that people will think we're "slacking" if we wander off in the woods.

Your frank self-assessment:
- Record your best memories of playing outside as a kid. What did you like to do? Where did you do it? What were the feelings associated with those times?
- What's your go-to place? Mountains? Ocean? Deep snow? Are you able to commit to a once-a-year immersion?
- Write down the ways you translate being in nature to reducing workplace stress. Should you be out more or less?

Flip's tips:
- Give yourself permission to regularly visit your own "sacred spot." My personal favorite is the "cathedral" forest—this is where the trees are so old, tall, and dense that they have shaded out much of the undergrowth, and it feels like I am indeed in church.
- Some of the best conversations happen when we are walking side by side through a natural landscape. Invite a colleague whom you want to know better for a stroll across the park or along the lake.
- Don't confuse outdoor exercise with your earbuds blasting while you think about work problems as being restorative time.

Action for traction:
- Although this may give you small shivers of anxiety, take a "digital detox" at least once a year. This means *at least* forty-eight hours with no cell phone, voice mail, e-mail, texting, or Internet. You'll be amazed at the positive things that will happen.
- See if you can get your organization to explore volunteer opportunities that will get you and your team outside. It can't hurt to ask!

- The next time you have some creative writing to do, do it outdoors in an inspiring setting. Office gray and beige just ain't natural!

Baked-in benefits:
- It's hard not to have appreciation for a larger view of life when we get out into the world.
- You may actually get some exercise.
- No one I know has ever said, "Gee, I should spend less time outdoors and more time in the office!"

For a deeper dive …
Anasazi Foundation. *The Seven Paths: Changing One's Way of Walking in the World.* Oakland, CA: Berrett-Koehler Publishers, 2013.

McDargh, Eileen. *Gifts from the Mountain: Simple Truths for Life's Complexities.* Oakland, CA: Berrett-Koehler Publishers, 2007.

… and on the Web:
"Cloudy with a Chance of Joy." TED Talks. June 2013. Accessed August 2, 2014. http://www.ted.com/talks/gavin_pretor_pinney _cloudy_with_a_chance_of_joy

Cortese, Alexa. "7 Reasons Why Spending Time in Nature Does Wonders for the Soul." *Huffington Post.* July 21, 2014. Accessed August 2, 2014. http://www.huffingtonpost.com/alexa-cortese/nature-health_b_5406030.html

Pretor-Pinney, Gavin. "Digital Detox: Disconnect to Reconnect." http://thedigitaldetox.org/

Weil, Andrew. "Eight Ways to Connect." Accessed August 2, 2014. http://www.drweil.com/drw/u/ART00591/Eight-Ways-To-Connect.html

NOTES AND NOODLINGS

CHAPTER 21

Connection to Spirit and the Sacred Mystery— You're Part of It, So Why Not Honor It?

"A soul-based workplace asks things of me that I didn't even know I had. It's constantly telling me that I belong to something large in the world."
—DAVID WHYTE

What it is ... Almost all of us feel that there is something "out there and in here" other than our normal, time-limited, material existence. While there are literally hundreds of names for what I will generically call a "Universal Life Force," what matters is not so much how we identify it (or argue about it), but how a positive connection to something we deem to be spiritual can enhance and enrich our lives.

Sample scenario #1: Tomás is not self-identified as a religious person; however, he has deep spiritual beliefs. One day, one of his colleagues asks him why he is seemingly able to handle the stress of work without the blaming and complaining that come from so many others. Tomás just smiles and says that work is just one way to be of service in his limited time here on the planet.

Sample scenario #2: Sally belongs to a faith-based organization that provides housing assistance. She would like to solicit contributions for their annual fundraising event, and carefully considers putting up some flyers at work and sending out an e-mail to her group. In the end, she decides to only invite those with whom she has a social relationship outside of the office.

Why will this help me at work? A greater sense of purpose, a belief in something greater than ourselves, and the ability to tap into a higher or deeper source of meaning can help us get through the workday with more grace and style.

Why is this so difficult at times? Spiritual beliefs must be carefully balanced, especially at work. Since we respect the diversity of all faiths and perspectives, we are all generally mindful about not imposing on others. And on the opposite end, we are uncomfortable when someone is trying to convert us to the way he or she believes.

Your frank self-assessment:
- When's the last time you sat down and reflected on what you truly believe? Where is there clarity versus confusion for you?
- What inherited patterns of religion, spirituality, or ritual do you still keep? Which ones have you reduced or eliminated? Are there any that are unique to you and your new family?
- What are the primary ways in which you put your beliefs into action? Where are there more opportunities?

Flip's tips:
- Check in with your personal belief system to see what the differentiation and overlaps are between what you view as religious versus spiritual.
- Find time for quiet. While there is spirit-in-action, there is tremendous benefit to taking some time for stillness in each day. This could be as simple as sitting quietly on a bench.
- Be spiritually humble, even though you may be unshakable in your beliefs.

Action for traction:
- Pick one practice or ritual that you know deepens your connection to spirit. Recommit to the consistency or depth of that practice.
- Take the risk—not at work!—to engage with someone who you know has very different spiritual beliefs. See what you can learn from him or her, and identify some areas of common ground.
- Write down two or three attributes of your spirituality, and then look for places in the coming week to "walk your talk" without anything resembling "preaching."

Baked-in benefits:
- You'll feel connected to a larger sense of purpose and meaning, at work and outside of work.
- You won't sweat the small stuff (and in almost every case, it is indeed small stuff).
- You'll radiate genuine positive vibes to those around you.

For a deeper dive …
Peppers, Cheryl, and Alan Briskin. *Bringing Your Soul to Work: An Everyday Practice.* Oakland, CA: Berrett-Koehler Publishers, 2000.

Singer, Michael A. *The Untethered Soul: The Journey Beyond Yourself.* Oakland, CA: New Harbinger Publications, 2007.

Thich Nhat Hanh. *Work: How to Find Joy and Meaning in Each Hour of the Day.* Berkeley, CA: Parallax Press, 2012.

… and on the Web:
Biali, Susan. "Helping You Find Your Life Purpose." *Psychology Today.* November 8, 2013. Accessed August 2, 2014. http://www.psychologytoday.com/blog/prescriptions-life/201311/helping-you-find-your-life-purpose

Kaizen Solutions. "Spirit at Work." Accessed August 2, 2014. http://www.kaizensolutions.org/saw.html

Karsan, Rudy. "Finding Meaning in Your Work." http://blog.kenexa.com/finding-meaning-in-your-work/

NOTES AND NOODLINGS

SECTION EIGHT

Balancing Self, Others, Work, and Life—Putting It All Reasonably Together

CHAPTER 22

Call It What You Will, It Takes Practice (So You Have to Have a Practice)

"Practice isn't the thing you do once you're good.
It's the thing you do that makes you good."
—MALCOLM GLADWELL

What it is … Concepts are great, knowledge is good, trying things out is helpful; however, for lasting change, we need to incorporate and integrate our new beliefs and behaviors through practice. Yoga, sports, meditation, music, and many other categories benefit from the commitment to consistency. Ideally, we practice not out of obligation or drudgery, but out of the set of enhanced feelings and experiences we get as a result of our dedication and diligence.

Sample scenario #1: When Alison gets stressed at work, she knows she has a choice. One is to head home for her favorite combo of junk food and junk TV. The other is to hit the dance movement class that she loves. Recently, she enlisted the help of a friend as an ally—when Alison goes to "junkville" (which she still may do from time to time), she gives $20 to her friend, who sends it to their favorite charity. More often, when she goes to dance class, she calls her friend later for an attagirl.

Sample scenario #2: Carlos has recently taken up aikido, and at first his coworkers made jokes about him coming in and throwing them down on the conference room floor. Soon, they realized that he is less reactive during meetings, more thoughtful in his responses, and more lighthearted. When they ask, Carlos says that his powers of concentration and compassion have improved as a result of this new endeavor.

Why will this help me at work? Having a healthy life skill that brings us balance, perspective, and joy can only be beneficial. Another aspect is

that most of us tend to be much less self-critical when we are engaged in a dedicated practice—does it really work to judge yourself harshly during yoga class? With any sort of practice, we hopefully increase our capacity for mindfulness, always a useful tool in the chaos of work.

Why is this so difficult at times? First, if you haven't noticed, we are still living in an instant-gratification culture. Second, technology can keep us flitting from input to input, with no real depth or value. Lastly, it takes faith that if we apply ourselves over time and persevere, we will obtain greater benefits than we might imagine.

Your frank self-assessment:
- What happens when you look at your commitment to a practice—do you see ongoing opportunity, or do you see "failure"?
- Where do you see a path that will bring you true benefits if you increase your dedication?
- What would a greater commitment look like for you, and how can you "make it so"?

Flip's tips:
- Find an individual or group who shares your practice. While many practices can be done alone, it is almost always a richer experience if we are able to give support to others and receive it in return.
- If you want a useful tool to reduce the internal chatter that keeps us from doing what is truly important (and not just urgent), try a meditation practice.
- Do something physical. There should be some practice that involves the healthy movement of the body, particularly if your butt is parked most of the day, like mine is.

Action for traction:
- Make six consecutive weekly appointments with yourself to "do your thing" (whatever it is). Do not allow yourself to cancel or no-show except in the case of a true emergency.
- Explain to your partner or family how important this practice is to you, and that you'd like their active support. Ask them what positive and negative trade-offs they would experience from you making a more significant effort in this way.
- Write up the job description of being a practitioner of your chosen method, and then list the benefits that come with the job.

Baked-in benefits:
- You'll have a greater sense of earned accomplishment.
- A better internal experience from day to day is certainly worth having.
- Virtually everyone reports increased balance and deeper satisfaction.

For a deeper dive …
Sterner, Thomas M. *The Practicing Mind: Developing Focus and Discipline in Your Life—Master Any Skill or Challenge by Learning to Love the Process.* Novato, CA: New World Library, 2012.

Williams, Mark, and Danny Penman. *Mindfulness: An Eight-Week Plan for Finding Peace in a Frantic World.* Emmaus, PA: Rodale Books, 2012.

… and on the Web:
Baime, Michael. "Practicing Mindfulness." PBS. Accessed August 2, 2014. http://www.pbs.org/thisemotionallife/blogs/practicing-mindfulness

"The Importance of Practice: Use it or Lose It." Accessed August 2, 2014. http://www.prolificliving.com/the-importance-of-practice-use-it-or-lose-it/

Prolific Living. "The Work as Meditation: How to Make Self-Inquiry a Steady Practice." http://www.theworkasmeditation.com/

NOTES AND NOODLINGS

CHAPTER 23

The Daily Integration of Our Inevitable Exit (Or, There Are Lots of Things Worse Than Dying)

"The fear of death follows from the fear of life. A man who lives fully is prepared to die at any time."
—MARK TWAIN

What it is ... You may be thinking. *Flip, I've been with you up to this point, but death? Talk about a buzzkill!* However, it's been said many times before across time and in almost every culture, our ability to live fully and completely requires us to live without fear of death. By holding the profound awareness that there is a limited time we have in this material form, we can make better use of the unknown amount we have. Unfortunately, our current society isn't there yet, but we can begin to, as David Whyte says, "apprentice ourselves to the art of our grand disappearance" (from his audio recording *What to Remember When Waking,* available from www. davidwhyte.com, or transcript available at http://www.soundstrue.com/ shop/What-to-Remember-When-Waking/2209.pdf).

Sample scenario #1: Joan is worried that she'll catch every new flu strain, that she'll be involved in an accident on the way to work, and that she is going to die before she's ready. This keeps her on an invisible and perpetual edge, which interferes with her ability to cope with stress and relax.

Sample scenario #2: Jonah had one uncle who was a minister, another who ran a funeral parlor. They were both pillars of comfort and care in the small town where he grew up. Jonah helped his uncle bathe and dress the deceased, and sat in the church as his other uncle brought meaning to the mourning. Jonah exhibits great empathy at his current workplace for those whose family members are dying or grieving, and does so with a gentle compassion that is wonderful to be around.

Why will this help me at work? Often when we face the death of a loved one or the news of our imminent demise due to a terminal illness, our priorities shift. Much of what passes for playing the game of business is just that—an interesting exercise. However, in the end, it is the positive impact that our work generates in the world that creates meaning. Knowing (and accepting) that we may leave this world at any time gives us a focus and depth that might not be there otherwise.

Why is this so difficult at times? Fear of death is deeply embedded in our American culture, yet at the same time, we are fascinated with movies that are full of it. We intellectually understand that we are physically finite beings; however, there is often a perpetual disconnect between that knowledge and our motivation to live a more purposeful life.

Your frank self-assessment:
- How comfortable are you discussing death and dying?
- Do you have your legal and financial affairs together? Would someone's life be majorly impacted if you were to die tomorrow because she would have to pick up a bunch of incomplete tasks?
- Do you have a theology or cosmology that helps put death in perspective for you?

Flip's tips:
- If you are uncomfortable around death, make an appointment to speak to a hospice nurse (you don't have to physically go there). Interview her or him about what her or his work is like, as if you were a reporter.
- If you have parents who are elderly or in poor health, think in advance about what role you would like to play in supporting them through their final chapters of growth.
- Find your favorite movie about the subject of death and dying (mine is *What Dreams May Come*) and watch it. Talk about it with some of your best buddies (if you dare).

Action for traction:
- If you are self-employed or in a leadership position, talk to those closest to you personally and professionally about what you would want them to do to carry on your legacy. Ask them what they need from you in order to make that happen.

- Become aware of the options in your community for care of the dying. Are there good options, or is there still a struggle for knowledge about palliative care and death with dignity?
- Have fun and write your own obituary. Plan your service, including the special music that you want. Write a letter to the mourners, cheering them on.

Baked-in benefits:
- You'll experience more ease from time to time.
- There will be a greater acceptance of the "big picture."
- Your business and family will thank you should the need arise.

For a deeper dive …

Butler, Katy. *Knocking on Heaven's Door: The Path to a Better Way of Death.* New York: Scribner, 2013.

Kessler, David. *The Needs of the Dying: A Guide for Bringing Hope, Comfort, and Love to Life's Final Chapter.* 10th anniv. ed. East Hampton, NY: Harper, 2007.

… and on the Web:

Brody, Jane E. "Facing Your Own Mortality." *New York Times.* October 9, 1988. Accessed August 2, 2014. http://www.nytimes.com/1988/10/09/magazine/facing-your-own-mortality.html? src=pm&pagewanted=1

Hanh, Thich Nhat. "No Death, No Fear: Excerpts." What-Buddha-Taught. Accessed August 2, 2014. http://www.dhammatalks.net/Books10/Thich_Nhat_Hanh_No_Death_No_Fear.htm

NOTES AND NOODLINGS

CHAPTER 24

Sustained Basic Goodness—How to Amaze and Delight Yourself as You Enjoy the Passage of Time

"Sometimes the light's all shining on me, other times I can barely see. Lately it occurs to me, what a long, strange trip it's been."
—THE GRATEFUL DEAD

What it is ... When we realize that instead of being helplessly strapped onto the roller coaster of life, we are actually the track codesigner, the ticket taker, and the maintenance worker, things shift. We have increased awareness in the moment of our patterns, triggers, and options. We tend to see things from an observer perspective, rather than a dramatic one. There is even a lighthearted approach to the stressors and hassles that used to wear us down. In short, while there is no shortage of challenges, we wake up eager to meet the day and lie down at night grateful for having experienced another one.

Sample scenario #1: Isabella has lost her mother, best friend, and a close coworker to cancer in the last two years. In addition, her house was seriously flooded in an epic storm, and one of her children was recently diagnosed with diabetes. Yet she appears to be one of the most well-adjusted people in the office. When a colleague asked her how she dealt with all the stress in her life, she replied, "I refuse to allow the circumstances of life to keep me from enjoying my life."

Sample scenario #2: Paul is the calm center of a chaotic workplace. He has the ability to shift the meetings back on track, to reach out to those who need extra assistance, and to somehow complete his work without always staying late or grumbling. He has many interesting and pithy sayings in his work space, one of them being "Experience is what you get when you don't get what you want."

Why will this help me at work? Being fully engaged yet able to practice the "art of healthy detachment," we are much more buoyant and resilient. This is not some New Age false bliss or convenient system of denial—it is being able to make a reasonable assessment of the current situation, examine our options, draw upon our support systems, and move through what's at hand without being handicapped.

Why is this so difficult at times? We all fall back into our old patterns—confusing work with old family crap, slipping into fault and blame, not finding the courage to enter into supportive confrontation, getting caught up in dysfunctional group dynamics. The list goes on …

Your frank self-assessment:
- Do you feel reasonably good more often than not?
- Can you catch yourself as you slide into negative states much of the time?
- Is there richness, contentment, and joy in your daily life?

Flip's tips:
- What we're talking about here is basically the full integration of your life—without perfectionism, self-judgment, or negativity. Your mission is to do the best you can.
- In order to assist in the raising of consciousness in your organization and with the people around you, it has to be authentically emanating from you, not from an ego-based place. So, continue to practice getting out of your own way.
- There is one factor that—as a general rule—increases our perspective and wisdom. I call it "more years on the planet" (also known as "getting older"). So, embrace the process of collecting wisdom.

Action for traction:
- Train yourself to find the place in your body that signals you when things start to tighten up or get weird. It can be tightness in the throat, a pressure on the chest, or a squirrelly stomach—these are our natural cues that we need to pay attention, that something is out of alignment in the present moment.
- If you don't have a good circle of five-gold-star peers, do what it takes to get them. I have a two-hour commitment every month with my Social Venture Network Peer Circle, and I would have to be in the hospital or jail to miss it—it's that valuable to me.

- Who wants what's best for you? Who wants what's best from you? A measure of true love is those wonderful people in our lives who both support us and challenge us. Give them your full attention and affection, and you'll be much better for it.

Baked-in benefits:
- When others experience that we can deal with virtually anything with skill, style, and grace, they generally deal with us differently and positively.
- Since there is no "future state of happiness"—only what we can experience now—there is no good reason to postpone your greater sense of fulfillment.
- When we fully embrace "If not you, then who? If not now, then when?" there is a sense of truly being the architect of our destiny.

For a deeper dive …
Cashman, Kevin. *Leadership from the Inside Out: Becoming a Leader for Life.* 2nd ed. Oakland, CA: Berrett-Koehler Publishers, 2008.

Whyte, David. *What to Remember When Waking* (audio). Available from www.davidwhyte.com, or transcript available at http://www.soundstrue.com/shop/What-to-Remember-When-Waking/2209.pdf

… and on the Web:
Good Life Project Blog. http://www.goodlifeproject.com/

Wallace, David Foster. "This Is Water" (transcription). 2005 Kenyon College Commencement Address. Accessed August 2, 2014. http://web.ics.purdue.edu/~drkelly/DFWKenyonAddress2005.pdf

Work Awesome Blog. Accessed August 2, 2014. http://workawesome.com/

NOTES AND NOODLINGS

CONCLUSION

One of the myths of life is that someday we'll "get there," as if magically all our striving toward health, happiness, and material satisfaction will crystallize in a final form. That illusion (or delusion) is hard to shake.

The reality is that we are continuously unfolding in our awareness, balance, and wisdom. There are many "dancing dichotomies"—dwelling in the duality of still striving yet totally accepting, knowing through the benefit of our experience and yet knowing how much we can't know, and connecting with others yet remaining in awe of the mystery of who they really are.

Each day provides an opportunity to take a fresh look, to tap into positive energy, and to actually do things differently. On a so-called "bad day," we curse ourselves and others, we feel that the world is against us, we chafe at restrictions, obstacles, and insensitivities.

What I have learned (correction—what I am still learning) is that I gain it and I lose it, and then I gain it and lose it again. The key for me is to bring my awareness into the present moment as often as I can so that my choices and actions are made out of consciousness, not just old patterns and habits.

At this point I have been extremely fortunate—and determined!—to be able to design and carry out a low-stress work life. Sure, I have my challenges, get my buttons pushed from time to time, and sometimes forget that I'm just havin' a spell of the blues (as opposed to being "less than").

What helps the most is three things: my unwavering commitment to personal and professional growth, my new rituals of practice, and most importantly, deepening the healthy relationships around me.

I hope that you can be your own best source of inspiration and change in a lighthearted, soulful way. "It all works out in the end, and if it hasn't, then obviously we're not at the end yet."

I wish you the best in all you do personally and professionally.

Flip

ADDITIONAL RESOURCES

I would not be as successful and satisfied professionally or personally without having had access to great resources over the years. I'll highlight the ones that I have found most valuable; however, feel free to send me an e-mail if you're interested in going deeper or further on a particular topic.

Your Support Network:

The opening line of David Whyte's poem "Everything Is Waiting for You" (from *Everything Is Waiting for You*, Many Rivers Press, 2003) goes "Your great mistake is to act the drama as if you were alone." Having a robust network of those who will both support you and challenge you cannot be overstated in terms of achieving the goals and methods outlined in this book. Here's how I differentiate among the categories of valuable supportive folks in my professional life:

Family and friends: Helpful, but limited, because of the histories and emotional investments. This reminds me of the country-western song "I Only Like Half the People I Love." They're good when they're truly there, but to do our deepest and most sustainable growth, we also need connections from the following categories ...

Peers: True peers are those who are equal partners in our dance of advancing our learning, working through our setbacks, and celebrating our progress. Peers have no financial interest, are not romantically involved (with us!), and can easily shift from listening to advocating. They can be open arrangements or structured. Here's an example of a conscious, dedicated model of peer support: http://svn.org/get-inspired/peer-circles

Mentor: A mentor is someone who has some accumulated knowledge and wisdom that he or she is willing to share with us to facilitate our growth. These are often, but not always, folks who have spent more time on the planet here (technology mentoring often being an exception). There is no financial compensation—otherwise it's something else—and we honor and respect our mentors with timeliness and gratitude.

Coach: A term that has come to represent a wide range of options in a growing field. Coaches can be "certified" or not, be area-of-expertise-specific or not, and be embedded in an organizational culture or not. Since

I do a lot of executive coaching (almost always in the context of a yearlong system-wide change effort), I am clear about the distinction between being a coach, a therapist, and a colleague. In my opinion, a coach who is compensated in a business context should have a set of goals and outcomes directly related to improved organizational results. While this is difficult to precisely measure, there should be a sense from both the client and those in his or her workplace that the patterns of behavior have changed and are being sustained. Certification as a coach demonstrates a certain commitment and comes with a set of ethical codes, but is no guarantee of effectiveness. Conversely, some of the best coaches eschew certification. Ask around—and ask a prospective coach for client references and his or her policies around confidentiality and payment.

Therapist: Good psychotherapy is invaluable, and perhaps the most challenging to find, obtain, and stay with. For me, one of the key features of this process is its ability—when done skillfully by therapist and client—to bring what is unconscious into consciousness. I would not be in the position of balance and success I am today without it. As someone who has been a Vermont Masters-level Licensed Psychologist for almost twenty years, I am still a member of this community, although I no longer provide therapeutic services. In terms of trying to find a good therapist, I use the analogy of scoping out a good chef. This person may make the best sushi in the world; however, if raw seafood doesn't work for you, it doesn't matter how skilled the chef is. As consumers we know about restaurants and we can see the menu in advance. Some therapists offer a wide range of treatment modalities, while others specialize. A counselor whom your friend raves about may not be a match for you.

The best approach in finding someone is to ask those people you admire (and believe me, virtually all those you look up to have probably been through the process) for suggestions. As Brené Brown has so successfully demonstrated through her books and TED Talks, vulnerability is a sign of strength, not weakness. When you meet with prospective therapists, ask them how they work, what their expectations are from you, and how the two of you would determine what's working. If you feel like this is someone who listens well, has genuine empathy, and is helpful, give it three sessions before you make your final determination.

As with coaches, what matters most is not their degrees, schools attended, or type of license—it is your direct experience of who they are in the room. Study after study has shown that the interpersonal connection with the therapist is the number-one factor in the clients' reports of success.

One thing that usually comes up in a good course of psychotherapy is some degree of anxiety. By design, we are seeking a guide who will help us go into the unknown—whether it be past, present, or future—and most of us stubbornly cling to what we know (because on some level it has worked well enough to get us here). This is why it takes a real commitment, especially when you think otherwise.

Organizations:

Social Venture Network (www.svn.org): The Social Venture Network is over twenty-six years old, and is a diverse and energetic group of around 650 national progressive businesses. I attend as many of their events as I can, and am always amazed and inspired at the ways in which creative SVN members are truly changing the world through their efforts.

B Lab (www.bcorporation.net): B Lab runs the nonprofit certification process for becoming a Certified B Corp (I became one in 2011) and working with state legislators to change incorporation laws so that they respect the multiple bottom-line approach to business. These folks are adding new B Corps on a weekly basis (now over 1,000), and you will hear and see more of this important initiative and its brand.

1% for the Planet (www.onepercentfortheplanet.org/en): A growing global movement founded by Yvon Chouinard from Patagonia of almost 1,400 companies that donate 1 percent of their sales to a network of 2,673 environmental organizations worldwide. Their motto is "Keep the earth in business," and I'm always happy to chip in my 1 percent.

Vermont Businesses for Social Responsibility (www.vbsr.org): VBSR is the largest organization of socially responsible businesses *in the country*, and provides education, advocacy, and networking, with over 1,100 members. I spent nine years (2002–2011) as a Board member, and am still an avid supporter. I'm proud of what we do here!

Retreat Centers:

As I referenced in the Acknowledgments, spending time at a retreat center, in a natural setting, where cell phones don't work, in a community of seekers and learners, is a fabulous way to take care of yourself and to restore and renew your mind, body, and spirit. Here are my favorites:

Esalen (www.esalen.org): Nestled on the Big Sur, California, coastline and considered the historical center of the "human potential movement," Esalen is a place with a rich history of thought and spirit leaders. They offer over six hundred workshops a year. It is located on a bluff right on the edge of the Pacific Ocean; I've soaked in the hot springs there looking out at the sea otters and dolphins playing in the ocean below, with whale spouts in the distance. They have an internationally famous massage school to boot. I try to go there every year if I can, and have been a workshop leader.

Breitenbush Hot Springs and Retreat Center (www.breitenbush.com): Located in the Cascade Mountains of Oregon, just off the road between Salem and Bend, it is a worker-owned cooperative with a unique governance structure. The site in the deep woods is off the grid—they have their own hydroelectric plant using the water from a mountain stream, and since they are sited on top of geothermal activity, they pump hot water from the ground to their cabins and lodge for heat. A geologist has calculated that the water emerging in the hot springs (and steam sauna) fell as snow sixty thousand years ago! I present a workshop here every May.

Hollyhock (www.hollyhock.ca): It takes a long time to get up to Cortes Island (six hours north of Vancouver, BC), but it sure is worth it once you get there. A sandy tidal beach, views of snowcapped mountains, and a lovely campus make Hollyhock a special experience. I particularly enjoy eating the oysters that are pulled fresh from the island's waters. Hollyhock is run by my good friends Dana Bass Solomon and Joel Solomon, and you should check out either the Social Change Institute or Social Venture Institute that occur every year.

Omega (www.eomega.org): Situated near Rhinebeck, New York, at the site of a former kids' camp, Omega draws major leaders of personal and institutional growth from around the world. I have attended workshops there since the early 1990s, and they continue to offer a highly varied catalog of interesting programs.

Whidbey (www.whidbeyinstitute.org): Whidbey Island is a lovely spot outside of Seattle, Washington, and while the Whidbey Institute has a smaller reach than some of the other retreat centers, it offers the local community a wonderful place for programs. David Whyte, a mentor, lives nearby, and I love to return to this special land. One of the cabins there has hand-carved animal faces peering out from the knotholes of a natural staircase—how wonderful!

INDEX

ABOUT THE AUTHOR

Flip Brown entered the world of work (and began his lessons about it) at the age of twelve in his father's independent grocery store. He went on to become a woodworker, a ski mechanic, an international business dude, a graduate student, an author, a mobile crisis team member, a nonprofit program director, a psychologist, an executive coach, a team facilitator, and a gigging musician, and has remained a lifelong learner and experience seeker.

Flip has a BA in Transpersonal Psychology from Burlington College and an MA in Counseling Psychology from Antioch New England Graduate School (now Antioch University New England). He has served as Adjunct Faculty at Antioch and Champlain College. He has had the privilege of learning from a number of gifted mentors, including the staff at the Jung Institute in Zurich, and Daniel Goleman, Edgar Schein, Marshall Goldsmith, Meg Wheatley, Roz and Ben Zander, and others. He serves on a small team working with David Whyte on his model of Conversational Leadership.

In 2000 he founded Business Culture Consultants, and it remains a solo practice assisting organizational owners, leaders, and managers to understand, change, and sustain their patterns of interaction and behavior. Put another way—he helps good people in great organizations get better results by having the conversations they really need to have but haven't figured out how to have on their own yet!

Business Culture Consultants (BCC) has been a longtime member of Vermont Businesses for Social Responsibility, was the fifth Certified B Corp in Vermont, and is a very active member of the Social Venture Network, where Flip serves as an Ambassador. BCC was recently listed as one of the top 10 percent of all B Corps in the area of Community Impact.

For more information, go to www.businesscultureconsultants.com

Flip lives close to Lake Champlain in Burlington, Vermont, with his wife, Sandy Post, and their stuffed bear, Ted. His interests include playing, listening to, and collecting vintage rock 'n' roll, growing (and eating) a large number of organic vegetables, all manner of winter sports (Alpine, telemark, and Nordic skiing, snowboarding), and the Finnish sauna. He feels blessed to have a rich, balanced life.

CONTACT INFO

For more information, including other options to purchase this book, updated resources, and further musings by the author, please visit:

www.balancedeffectiveness.com

To contact Flip directly, e-mail him at author_flip@icloud.com, or send a tweet to @FlipBrownVT.

He'd love to hear from you!

Open Book Editions
A Berrett-Koehler Partner

Open Book Editions is a joint venture between Berrett-Koehler Publishers and Author Solutions, the market leader in self-publishing. There are many more aspiring authors who share Berrett-Koehler's mission than we can sustainably publish. To serve these authors, Open Book Editions offers a comprehensive self-publishing opportunity.

A Shared Mission

Open Book Editions welcomes authors who share the Berrett-Koehler mission— Creating a World That Works for All. We believe that to truly create a better world, action is needed at all levels—individual, organizational, and societal. At the individual level, our publications help people align their lives with their values and with their aspirations for a better world. At the organizational level, we promote progressive leadership and management practices, socially responsible approaches to business, and humane and effective organizations. At the societal level, we publish content that advances social and economic justice, shared prosperity, sustainability, and new solutions to national and global issues.

Open Book Editions represents a new way to further the BK mission and expand our community. We look forward to helping more authors challenge conventional thinking, introduce new ideas, and foster positive change.

For more information, see the Open Book Editions website:
http://www.iuniverse.com/Packages/OpenBookEditions.aspx

Join the BK Community! See exclusive author videos, join discussion groups, find out about upcoming events, read author blogs, and much more! http://bkcommunity.com/

CPSIA information can be obtained at www.ICGtesting.com
Printed in the USA
BVOW05s1727061014

369663BV00002B/8/P